June 2009

Nicola

Blessings

Debbie Z.

Zibu
THE POWER OF
ANGELIC SYMBOLOGY

By
Debbie Zylstra Almstedt, ATP

SECOND EDITION
First Printing, 2007

Artwork by Debbie Zylstra Almstedt
Cover design by Pat Brier, www.patriciabrier.com

Library of Congress Control Number: 2007920538
Almstedt, Debbie Zylstra—
    Zibu: The Power of Angelic Symbology /
Debbie Zylstra Almstedt—1ˢᵗ ed.

        c.   cm.
        ISBN: 978-0-9798302-0-4
        Library of Congress Control Number: 2007920538

Debbie Zylstra Almstedt
P.O. Box 55751
Shoreline, WA 98155

www.languageofzibu.com

Dedication

To my loving husband and spiritual partner, Johan, who has never given up believing in me, and to my beautiful daughter, Alexandra, my Earth Angel, who continually teaches me new lessons.

Acknowledgements

This information is available because of the guidance I have received from my lovely Angels and Guides, including Zephyrine, Zimone and Zebus. I am delighted to share their messages.

I will always be grateful to Laura Lees, Reiki practitioner, for being instrumental in my making connection with my Angelic Guides and for being there when I first heard the words about Zibu Angelic symbols.

This project came together smoothly due to the assistance I received from publisher Shelley Kaehr, and for that, I will always be filled with gratitude. Thanks to Linnea Armstrong for her editing and formatting skills.

I also thank my dear friend Jane Li for her continued support and words of encouragement.

Contents

The Symbols of the Angelic Realm

"Zibu symbols open up
energetic portals
for
Heavenly transformation."

—Angel Zephyrine

Angel Zephyrine's Message

When I asked Angel Zephyrine what was most optimal to tell people about the symbols, this is what I received:

"Let them know these will assist them in awakening to their true purpose in being on this Earth Plane at this time. The effects of Zibu will be felt worldwide. It will have far-reaching effects. One need but hold or behold the symbols to begin the awakening process.

"The banner and the signs with symbols [that Debbie uses at her booth] are enough to make people begin to remember. The language will help Humans to remember their Divine role on this Earth Plane. All Humans have important roles to play. They have forgotten and the symbols will re-ignite the memories.

"The frequency level of the language will remove the veils which keep Humans from seeing clearly and remembering their places—their roles. All roles fit together as puzzle pieces. When Humans awaken, they will know how they fit into the puzzle of life. They will remember which role they signed up to play. The Harmony created by reconnecting with one another will have a tremendous impact on the world.

"As the pieces fit together, the energy level will increase. It will be unmistakable. All will see and hear and feel it and will find their place in the scope of the Big Picture. This is an important step for mankind. All problems and superficial trappings will fall by the wayside as mankind embraces what is true and real.

"This is about how Humans fit into the Universal image—the grand scale of things. The language holds many answers for mankind. The symbols are the keys to the future. They unlock the tight grip that has held Humans in bondage. Once awakening begins, there will be no stopping it.

"The language is at the core of all things. It is at the center of the spiral. It is at the center of the Universe. These are keys to open the locked memories. It will unfold beautifully as those who awaken take their places for the 'Grand Re-Opening'—the Grand Re-Birth.

"Your reception [Debbie's] has been fine-tuned to receive greater information and relay it as concisely as possible. The information will be condensed into the symbols which will carry the information to the recipients.

"People are awakening as they begin to see and notice the written symbols. Once awakened, they will not be catatonic again. It is not reversible. It will spread like wild fire. There will be no stopping the mass awakening. It will be an awakening high and above the superficial level lives have been lived at previously. Unnecessary items will fall away and lose their importance. Truth will be recognized. There will be a clear path to Truth for all.

"The dominoes have begun to tumble. There is no stopping the process.

"Blessings."

Symbology

The focus of this book is on the power of Angelic symbology, and the Angels provided clarification with the following definition:

"Symbology is a method of infusing energy into a space. It has properties that go beyond the visual. They are instrumental in setting intentions. Symbols hold energy and also act as methods of transmitting energy. They hold space. They act as visual cues of what is happening on a non-visible level. Symbols transcend speech. They need not be spoken as they can be universal and convey meanings to those on many levels. Angelic symbols carry 'Divine connections.' It is effortless. It is a conduit to bring direct connection to the Angelic Realm."

Introduction

This has been a transformative time for me, as I move away from an ego-driven life and awaken to the possibilities that I can be of assistance to others. After spending 25 years as a secretary, doing the only form of work of which I thought I was capable, I began to awaken and remember why I'm here on this earth plane.

After leaving the corporate world in 1998, I began to express myself through art. I had always enjoyed various forms of art as a hobby, but this new expression came at a time when I needed to examine why I was showing up each day.

I had experimented with stained glass, calligraphy, pen and ink drawing, and painting. I even considered being a graphic designer and enrolled in art school at age 25. Burned out by persistent failed efforts at perfection, I dropped out after 2-1/2 years, convinced I was doomed to be a drone typing at a computer. I worked hard at doing and saying and being what was expected of me as I molded myself into the Executive Secretary role. I was doing what I thought I was meant to do for a living, but I was sad and empty inside with failing health.

When I was laid off from my last Executive Secretary job, I thought it was the worst thing that could have possibly happened. Thoughts of revising my resume and psyching myself up for job interviews were disheartening to say the least.

With that first unemployment check, I chose to buy some wire to experiment with and do some art therapy. I enrolled in some wire working classes, and discovered that the wire was a great medium to work with. It was a magical experience to transform unruly bundles of wire into graceful fluid pieces of jewelry.

This was how I fulfilled my creative needs, but my ego was still very much attached. As I designed and made jewelry, I soon discovered that people were willing to pay money and purchase it. This was very exciting, indeed. However, when ego is attached and very much present, it can be discouraging when others don't share the same enthusiasm or positive view. It became clear to me that my artwork was an extension of me. When I made my jewelry available to the public, I felt that the very core of my self was on naked display to receive a confirmation of worthiness or lack of worth. How could I continue to look outside myself for an indication of whether I was okay or not? The answers would soon come in an unexpected manner.

An acquaintance introduced me to a group of spiritually-minded people who met weekly to explore ways to live at our highest potential. We learned to connect to Universal Consciousness. I made my first pendulum and was taught how to use this tool to receive yes/no answers to my carefully worded questions.

It seemed that I made very slow progress as I got simple yes and no answers and witnessed others quickly advancing to a place where they would "hear" or "know" Truth from Spirit, God, Universal Consciousness... call it what you will.

I am often baffled by my frustration at not making faster personal growth and am always surprised when I see who has been obstructing my way, as it is always me. "Hey, who's been in my way all this time?" "Who has been blocking my path?" I am quick to forget that when I look outside of myself for answers, I'm disappointed. The answers lie within. When I get out of my own way, things flow much easier.

When I relaxed and looked within and avoided comparing to others, more gifts arrived.

The Artist's Way

Many times I had attempted to do the reading assignments and exercises in Julia Cameron's book *The Artist's Way*. The book sat on my bookshelf for years and periodically I would take it down and give it a feeble attempt. As I talked with others I came in contact with, I discovered that many of them, too, had the book and had valiantly begun the process only to abandon their well-meaning efforts one or two chapters into the book.

What I needed was a partner to commit to doing the 12-chapter process along with me. By being held accountable to another artist, I found myself sticking to the path. My artist friend and I completed the book in 13 weeks, having only skipped one week.

The purpose of the study was to eliminate the blocks which stifle creativity. I was guided to do Morning Pages, which consisted of writing a minimum of three pages long-hand of whatever came to mind. This was a brilliant method to release unnecessary mind chatter and clutter to get to the creativity. A variety of weekly assignments throughout the book were given as methods of refilling the often-depleted "creative well" with new visual images or stimulating sounds.

At the end of the 13 weeks, I looked forward to writing each morning in my journal with the flowing ink from my cherished fountain pen. Then a curious thing happened. I could see my handwriting change. It slowly began to appear loopier. It was reminiscent of when I was ten years old and would dot my "i's" with circles. It was a lazy, flowing, contented style of writing. The descenders on my y's and g's became exaggerated and extended to spirals. In fact, many letters adopted this distinguishing feature.

Then one morning while writing in my journal, I turned the page to continue writing and wrote what looked very much like the shorthand symbols from years earlier. The symbols were clear and beautiful. I wrote pages of these symbols— they would repeat at times and then continue into new symbols.

It puzzled me because the symbols were not shorthand forms, but they looked familiar somehow and they gave me a strong sense of comfort. The repetition of drawing these new symbols brought me much joy and yet I had no idea what they meant or where they came from.

The Reiki Treatment

Laura is a Reiki practitioner from whom I had received several energy treatments. Throughout each session, we would both see colors and shapes and movements. We talked to each other during the treatments as we compared notes.

Weeks after I began drawing the mysterious symbols, I made an appointment with Laura. The session proceeded as usual with me lying on the massage table with my eyes closed, as Laura directed Reiki energy throughout my body with her hand placement. I saw beautiful colors and shapes, but was caught off guard when a face slowly appeared. I was concerned because I didn't know what it was. I whispered to Laura that someone was with me and was talking to me. This face was stunningly beautiful as a Greek god or goddess. It wasn't male or female, although I often will refer to it as "she" because of the gentle energy I sensed.

I lay quietly on the table and listened while this gorgeous being told me the following:

"What you have been drawing, Dear Debbie, is an Angelic healing language called Zibu. We invite you to be a messenger and share this with mankind. We also invite you to express these symbols in silver wire as jewelry. This will be your initial voice to share the messages."

It was then that I realized it was an Angel who had appeared before me and not a ghost, as I had initially thought. This was quite different from the images in books and paintings which portray Angels in flowing gowns with ribbons and glorious wings.

This was not like anything I had experienced before. I was in shock. An Angel had just appeared out of nowhere and spoken to me. I was being asked to share the symbols and messages with mankind. Mankind! This request reflected a much larger scale than merely mentioning it in passing to my family and close friends. I wasn't sure at this point whether I should tell anyone...and risk having them think I was deranged. This was going to take a while to digest.

Within three weeks, three major events changed my life. The Angel's appearance was the beginning of this series of events. Automatic writing was the next. I had read about automatic writing and found myself trying desperately to experience watching my beloved fountain pen fly furiously over paper to reveal messages. I tried so hard. I know that I was, again, in my own way. Once I relaxed, it happened with ease a week after the visit from the Angel.

I would write a question and then wait for an answer to come through. Unlike my vision of having my hand yanked around uncontrollably, this was very gentle. I would hear the message and simultaneously write it out. My own handwriting was of moderate size on lined paper; however, the messages I received were much larger and fast-moving. I was fully aware of what I was writing, but was often surprised as I re-read the information. It was as fresh as reading it for the first time.

I might add at this point that I made it a practice to begin these sessions with a prelude which was:

"I remove any and all blocks. I release attachment to outcome. I acknowledge my ego and ask that ego step aside as a silent observer and partner with me so we may receive clear, true and accurate information only from those who shine in Spirit's pure white light."

This set the stage to receive Truth. It also released my attachment to controlling the information. I know from experience that when using a pendulum, I can be attached to the outcome. If I want a "yes" answer to the question of whether I should eat a piece of chocolate—I can make myself receive a "yes."

When I first used this process, I must admit that it didn't feel good to imagine shoving my ego aside. So I adjusted my mental picture. The image I now see is a tranquil gazebo floating over my left shoulder. This gazebo is filled with luxurious fluffy pillows. As I ask my ego to step aside, I visualize my ego having a lovely break and relaxing in a place of beauty rather than being harshly cast aside. It works for me—and makes me smile every time.

The third change that happened for me was internalizing my pendulum. I was fascinated by the ability to use the body as a pendulum. I had witnessed others who would spontaneously move an index finger for affirmative and a pinky for negative. Other more vigorous responses included full body movement of rocking forward and back while seated in a chair for "yes" or wiggling left and right for "no."

Relying on a pendulum was not what I wanted—so I requested a physical answer to my questions. Initially I had to relax my jaw and take a few deep breaths to calm my body. I was ecstatic when my head began to nod vigorously for "yes." It was only mildly embarrassing, however, that I felt I resembled Mr. Ed, the talking horse from the 1960's TV show, who would nod his head in an exaggerated fashion while talking to his owner.

This eventually calmed down to the discreet modified head nod for "yes" and quick left and right movement for "no." For emphasis, I sometimes receive a succession of three quick emphatic nods as if the Angels are saying, "yes, yes, yes...this is definitely correct."

Now I was prepared to make significant progress with: 1) the understanding that I was drawing an Angelic healing language; 2) automatic writing to receive detailed messages; and 3) the ability to confirm the accuracy of the information utilizing my internalized pendulum.

One by one, I began to translate the pages of symbols from my journal. I am impressed even now with the gentle nature of the Angelic energy. The Angels always deliver their messages with enormous amounts of love, patience, and kindness.

For many years in the corporate world I had been characterized as being "too sensitive" and "thin-skinned." It is clear to me now that it is this same sensitivity which has contributed to my ability to receive these gentle messages from the Angelic Realm, and for that I am truly grateful.

In fact, as I begin each day, I take time to give thanks for all my blessings. Even on those days when outward illusions may paint a negative picture, I say "thank you Dear Spirit for all my Blessings." As I say this aloud, I draw the Zibu symbol for Gratitude three times in the air with my fingers.

This simple gesture is enough to shift my focus from anything negative or worrisome to a place of gratitude—for there are always Blessings to acknowledge.

Deciphering the Symbols

With my journal in hand, I would ask, "Which symbol do you want me to learn about next?" As I let my eyes glide over a page of 60 symbols, there would always be one that would seem to have a white glow around it. While pointing to it, I would ask, "Is this the one?" and my head would invariably nod "yes." "If you want me to be a messenger, please tell me what your message is," I would prompt them. In my quiet mind, I would clearly hear the Angels whisper the word "Courage" or "Healing" or "Tranquility." Over time, the messages have evolved into more flowing sentences, as the information streams in.

The information I have received about each symbol expanded to include the associated gemstones, colors, and places on the human body. The specified gemstones and colors amplify the energy of the symbols when they are combined. The part of the body is noted to assist in finding the most optimal symbol when energetically treating a specific physical issue. Those who already do Reiki energy work are especially encouraged to see if the symbols can add more dimension to their work.

The Angels and I urge you to use your intuition and to experiment with the symbols. Be playful and have fun with these as you find your own ways to express them and experience their wondrous healing effects.

The Symbols of the Angelic Realm

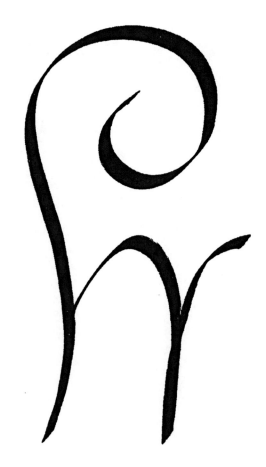

Abundance

Zibu translation: "Rama" (rah'-mah)
Color: Black
Gemstone: Carnelian
Physical Body: Lower Leg

"Abundance covers many aspects of life. It is the grandness of Life. It is all of the Blessings in Life. Abundance comes to those who ask. It is available to all. Release expectations and open your arms to receive. All will flow to you in Divine Right Order. Abundance touches every aspect of Life. There is much to embrace."

—Blessings from the Angels

The way I originally saw this symbol is reflected here. However, at a later point, it was elaborated upon with three dashes off to the side and the meaning was adjusted to "unlimited abundance." This is shown later in the book.

There are a multitude of ways to utilize this symbol. It is a great symbol to draw on the outside of your checkbook. The important aspect is setting a clear intention about what kind of abundance you are asking for. Is it for an abundance of money, clients, or friends? As you sit with this image of abundance, see in your mind's eye that which you are willing to attract into your life. Infuse that image with the actual symbol of abundance. It can be drawn in your mind, in the air with your fingertips, or you can write out your affirmation and include the symbol. Set your intention, watch for the results to show up, and thank the Angels for their assistance in manifestation.

Acceptance of Optimum Health

Zibu translation: "Hatumi" (hah-too'-mee)
Color: Green
Gemstone: Turquoise
Physical Body: Circulatory System

"Breathe life into your body and envision it as the healthy temple it is intended to be. Breathe deeply and bring oxygen to your blood. It will deliver the life-supporting elements to elevate your body's experience. See yourself as a thriving being with all components working together as one and functioning fully and completely. It is as it was meant to be. See it as being so."
—Blessings from the Angels

This symbol has a special place in my heart, as I used it to help my husband when he was in need.

In 2005, he was diagnosed with a rare form of cancer. It was a tremendous shock to my whole family, and I felt especially helpless in knowing how to support him through this ordeal. He was hospitalized several times over the course of six months, and my focus was calling upon the Angels to assist my dear husband.

His casts were changed regularly over the course of several weeks, and I was guided to adorn them with Zibu symbols to infuse Angelic healing energy. It was a treat for me to answer the doctors' questions about what they were, even though they really didn't understand. Since I see Angelic energy as golden in color, I also drew a series of symbols with a gold pen on a long strip of fabric that my husband could hold in his hands. He told me many times that this gave him reassurance and reminded him of the presence of the Angels.

The symbol for Acceptance of Optimum Health was the one I was guided to use on his pillowcase. It was drawn in emerald green in fabric paints on a white pillowcase that made its trip to the hospital each time another stay was required.

I knew in my heart that I was making a unique connection through the Zibu symbols to bless him and assist in his healing. My husband has made a full recovery and is thriving beautifully!

Authenticity

Zibu translation: "Asi" (ah'-see)
Color: Blue
Gemstone: Sodalite
Physical Body: Solar Plexus

"Authenticity is a sincere trueness to one's original blueprint. Being authentic is a genuine expression of the very core of your being. It is a refusal to deny who you are. This clear image is the most pure love and light-filled expression of your true nature. It expresses a richness and bountifulness not otherwise shown. Its luminosity glows and shines light on all who come in contact."
—Blessings from the Angels

A very good friend of mine regularly calls upon the Angels using the Zibu symbols. She also wears one of her many Zibu necklaces on a daily basis.

It was no surprise to me that when she was inspired to get a second tattoo, she chose an Angelic symbol. As she settles more and more into her authentic expression of who she is at her very core, I see the assistance she has received through contact with the Angels via the symbols.

We both received the same information about which symbol would be most optimal for her, and we concurred about the location. She now sports a beautiful cobalt blue tattoo of the authenticity symbol on the top of her foot along with the words "I am." She has reported that the energy is, indeed, palpable. I see it as highly significant as she steps forward on her life path completely committed to expressing her authentic self.

Awakening
Zibu translation: "Huka" (hoo'-kah)
Color: Yellow
Gemstone: Clear Quartz
Physical Body: Shoulders

"The awakening we refer to is not a physical awakening, but an opening of One's Heart and Soul to hear and accept and express Truth. It is an embracing of that which does not change. It is an awakening to the mysteries of life on the earth plane. The gifts derived from an awareness of the clarity of thought and pureness of Heart are far-reaching. There is enormity in the benefits of being willing to look within and see clearly all that is true."

—Blessings from the Angels

There are many ways to use each of the symbols in this book. I can see this symbol embellishing a meditation area. The symbol could be painted on the wall or on a banner as a visual cue of one's willingness to open up and receive information from within.

I recall a day when I painted Angelic symbols on the wall of a woman's Reiki treatment room. I was eager for her to experience the powerful energy as she watched me call in the Angels and have them infuse their energy as I painted.

What I discovered was that as the painter, I felt the profound energy through my whole being and could barely finish the tenth and final symbol as I was so overcome with emotion. The finished result was stunning, and the presence of the Angels and their healing energy was unmistakable.

Please know that your own experience will be unique to you, but will undoubtedly be powerful in its own way.

Balance

Zibu translation: "Himu" (hee'-moo)
Color: Yellow
Gemstone: Fluorite
Physical Body: Chest

"Balance is at the core. Balance leads the way. It will provide guidance when listening to the Heart. Balance resides in the Heart. That is where the messages are. Balance is necessary for survival. Please listen to it. Keep it in the Heart to stay on the path. Watch for reminders in life daily. They are all around."
—Blessings from the Angels

The symbol for balance is especially useful when you are feeling pulled in many different directions. At times when you feel the restless urge to dash to one extreme or another, this symbol can bring you back to center. When this symbol shows up during a reading, it is an indication that the person may be focusing too much time on work and not enough time on play or that some other aspect of their life is not in harmony. When referencing this symbol, the Angels may show me an image in my mind of someone racing from the far left to the right and back again, or an uneven scale showing more weight to one direction or the other.

In situations like this, consider the value of spending some time with this symbol. Slow down and draw the symbol, or imagine it being drawn on your chest, which is the associated part of the body. This symbol is one that I draw on the back of my hand as a reminder when things are feeling out of balance for me. It has the power to provide a sense of coming back to your core and allowing you to feel alignment once again.

Beacon of Hope

Zibu translation: "Sati" (sah'-tee)
Color: Yellow
Gemstone: Clear Quartz
Physical Body: Hands

"Kindness is shared with many as one becomes a Beacon of Hope. Direct contact is not necessary for one to shed light for others. Standing tall and confidently on one's path can provide encouragement and hope for others. Expressing one's authenticity and passion for life is a beautiful way to illuminate the darkness perceived by those around you. Shine brightly as many more beacons are needed to assist your fellow beings."

—Blessings from the Angels

The Angels always provide a rich, vivid image when I see this symbol. I am shown a beacon with a stunningly bright light. I see it gently washing over everyone it comes in contact with flooding them with unconditional love, acceptance and encouragement.

When I prepare to give readings, or present a lecture or class, I always ask the Angels to infuse me with their light, so I can be of service to others and be a Beacon of Hope.

Beauty
Zibu translation: "Arani" (ah-rah'-nee)
Color: Black
Gemstone: Lapis
Physical Body: Liver

"Beauty comes from the Soul. It is not visual. It is felt. It is understood. It is much more than it is believed to be. Beauty is deep within. It is Spirit expressing Itself in human form. Beauty is a deep well with much to bring forward. It is true expression of Spirit. It sustains us all. Beauty is action and intent. It reflects like water. It is deep like a well."

—Blessings from the Angels

Synchronicity fascinates me. The way that specially-timed events unfold with guidance from Spirit always fills with me with delight. This was true when I participated in a large metaphysical expo a few years ago.

As a petite elderly Jamaican woman wandered into the conference room, I noticed her immediately. She was reserved and had an interesting attire of mismatched clothing. As she approached my booth, she seemed hesitant to give any information about herself when I tried to strike up a conversation.

Once she had taken time to scan the Zibu symbols, she asked me to tell her about them, which I did. Then she asked me to look at her and tell her what I saw. If this had happened many years ago, I would have only seen the outward physical appearance and would have been at a loss for words.

In that moment when I really looked into her eyes, I was overwhelmed from head to toe with a high vibrational feeling. I was in awe looking at this small-statured unassuming woman. It took me a few moments to articulate my emotional response. I explained that I saw "intense beauty" and that I felt honored to be in her presence. I kept seeing the symbol for beauty over and over in my mind. She smiled and told me that her name was Beauty. I drew out the symbol for her, and have no doubt that she is here on the earth plane with a very special assignment.

Begin Anew

Zibu translation: "Hakuma" (hah'-koo-mah)
Color: Blue
Gemstone: Rose Quartz
Physical Body: Cellular Structure

"We invite you to Begin Anew by stepping through the threshold of Truth. The Truth holds the answers for you and will set you free. The new life you are invited to embrace is filled with Blessings and Love and Compassion. As you embrace these qualities, doors will open for you. Your path will become more clear. Your vision will not be clouded any more."

—Blessings from the Angels

There is one room in my home that is dedicated as a quiet room primarily for meditation. To set that intention, my family and I painted it a fresh new color of blue. Then we each took turns embellishing the walls and infusing our loving energy.

My husband is interested in astrology, so he painted his meaningful symbols in a silver glaze. Then our daughter added her special touch with small hearts and stars. I finished by calling upon the Angels to bless the room as I painted Begin Anew and other Zibu symbols in a gold glaze. Upon completion of our project, we basked in the quietude of the oasis we had collectively created.

It has quickly become the favorite spot in the house, and our cats even found it to be a calm and nurturing place to hang out.

Blessings

Zibu translation: "Sima" (see'-mah)
Color: Green
Gemstone: Fluorite
Physical Body: Crown Chakra

"Blessings flow from the unseen to manifest in great Beauty. Blessings are a regular occurrence, and we encourage a watchful eye and attentive Heart to see and feel the many Blessings that surround all. An expression of gratitude for existing Blessings brings an even greater abundance. Open your awareness to the splendor that surrounds you. That which you focus upon will be magnified."
—Blessings from the Angels

During Angel readings, there are times I see a ring around the client created by the repetition of the symbol for blessings. This is how the Angels get my attention and ask that I remind the person that they are surrounded by blessings but are unaware of them. The client is asked to reflect upon those precious gifts that are present, and by doing so, more blessings will appear. What we focus upon will be magnified. This is primarily a reminder to wake up and appreciate and acknowledge what is already present, so more of the same will arrive.

The symbol for Blessings is also one of my favorites to send to others. I love to draw symbols on envelopes of letters to friends, as well as when I pay my bills. This is an excellent symbol to use for this purpose, as it blesses the recipient, and brings wonderful energy to postal workers who deliver or handle the mail.

It always brings a smile to my face as I send these symbols out into the world, knowing that other's lives will be touched in a loving and positive way.

Buoyancy

Zibu translation: "Haka" (hah'-kah)
Color: Red
Gemstone: Clear Quartz
Physical Body: Toes

"Buoyancy is a beautiful feature. It allows one to float above the negativity. Buoyancy floats above that which is heavy. Negativity can weigh one down. It is dense and heavy. Buoyancy is achieved through embracing the positive and the light. Once buoyancy is shared, others will also experience the lightness and come to the surface. Reach out to others to connect the buoyancy."
—*Blessings from the Angels*

The symbol and message for buoyancy convey a beautiful image of a life preserver or flotation device. I see lower vibrational energies as dark and heavy. Imagine how the heavy energies of thoughts like fear and hatred can weigh a person down. That is the time to turn to the light and the higher vibrational thoughts of love and gratitude. Symbols for Love and Gratitude can be useful in situations like these, or even the symbol for Buoyancy.

Celebration

Zibu translation: "Akutu" (ah'-koo-too)
Color: White
Gemstone: Pearl
Physical Body: Arms

"Every moment of every day is a time for celebration. Give thanks, express gratitude for the Beauty and Love in Life. Expressing your Divine nature is reason enough to celebrate. Share this energy—this passion for Life. It is contagious in a most glorious manner. It can spread quickly and warm the Hearts of multitudes. This kind of celebration costs nothing, but brings richness to many."
—Blessings from the Angels

One client of mine was in an on-again off-again relationship that was not a healthy one. When she finally woke up to the fact that she deserved better treatment and ended the relationship, she came to me for a necklace with a symbol. This symbol quickly showed up along with a loving message for her to celebrate this new passion for a healthy lifestyle. In addition, as the Angels said, "every moment of every day is a time for celebration." It is a reminder to live life to the fullest every day knowing that this passion for life is contagious and enriches the lives of those we come in contact with...either directly or indirectly. What a beautiful gift!

Centeredness

Zibu translation: "Akunata" (ah-koo-nah'-tah)
Color: Orange
Gemstone: Carnelian
Physical Body: Heart

"The symbol for Centeredness brings the focus to one's core. The core is the point of balance. Finding this place of centeredness is of great assistance in moving forward effortlessly. There is no need to run into obstacles or meet resistance when one is centered. It is a place of power. It is place to recharge one's energy—to revitalize—to refocus. Centeredness will allow one to leap forward with sure-footedness and security and steadiness."

—Blessings from the Angels

On days when I feel pulled in many directions and unfocused, I have found this symbol to be indispensable.

Coming to a complete stop is helpful, as I focus on the energy of this symbol. It gives me a visual image of pulling back to the center of my being and rebalancing myself. I may draw it in the air with my fingertips or on paper repeatedly as I settle down to refocus.

I have discovered that I am much more effective when I take time to do this. Try it. It works!

Choose Life

Zibu translation: "Rasini" (rah'-see-nee)
Color: White
Gemstone: Clear Quartz
Physical Body: Skeletal System

"Please know that the symbol for Choose Life comes with enormous power to eradicate joy-less living. This symbol brings with it a real knowing of the importance of embracing life fully. It awakens the Soul. It ignites the passion again. It allows the Heart to re-joice—to know Joy again. Begin anew with this precious symbol, which awakens the Soul to be fully present and fully alive."
—Blessings from the Angels

When I was first invited by the Angel at the Reiki session to make jewelry in the shape of the symbols, it was specified to be in silver. A couple years after that first encounter, this symbol was revealed to me along with guidance to create it in gold. This indicated to me that the vibration of this symbol marked a switch to a higher level of energy.

What I received was that this symbol had enormous power to assist the majority of the population. Millions of people mechanically go through their daily lives in a detached manner. When one chooses life, or embraces life, it is a key to be fully awake in the present moment...the Now.

Also, when lives are consumed with fears and concerns about the future along with regrets about the past, then the joys of the present moment can be lost. This symbol is a magnificent reminder of staying present in the moment and noticing all the details which enrich life.

Clarity of Purpose

Zibu translation: "Rakumi" (rah-koo'-mee)
Color: Red
Gemstone: Bloodstone
Physical Body: Integumentary System (skin, hair and nails)

"This Angelic symbol brings with it the ability to receive Clarity about one's purpose in being on the Earth Plane at this time. The clarity comes with the enhanced connection to the Angelic Realm. Ask the questions you hold in your Heart and feel the answers come to the surface. Take time to look within and relax knowing the answers are close at hand. Embrace the Beauty of the knowledge that flows with ease to you. See with clarity what unfolds before you as you continue to ask for and receive clarity."

—Blessings from the Angels

During Angel readings, I am often asked by my clients what their life purpose is. Sometimes generalities are revealed to me to be shared, and other times I am shown this symbol. This is an excellent symbol to sit with and meditate. It provides a direct connection with the Angel realm. I am reassured by the Angels that when the client is ready and willing to open up and hear for themselves, the answers will be provided loud and clear. The key is the sincerity of the question and whether the client is actually willing to hear what is offered.

There is a gentle power in drawing the symbol either in the air or on paper, or even tracing the symbol in the book with one's finger. This repetitive movement will free the mind, helping it to quiet down and actually hear the inspirations being whispered by the Angels.

Even when trying to discern clear direction on a non-life-purpose issue, this is a valuable tool to gain clarity in moving forward on a project.

Compassion
Zibu translation: "Noti" (noh'-tee)
Color: Blue
Gemstone: Citrine
Physical Body: Head

"Compassion is a way of life. It connects the points in life. It connects Heart and Soul. It brings joy. It is healing. Compassion blends the layers. It responds to touch. It opens the Heart. It allows Love in. Compassion for oneself and for others. It realizes Truth. It hears the Truth. It unites. It combines. It brings people together. It has much power. Share compassion with yourself and others. It will make a world of difference."

—Blessings from the Angels

One of the reasons this symbol appears during a reading is as a reminder of compassion for oneself. I have met many people who are kind and compassionate, who don't hesitate to help others. They can give to others without a second's hesitation.

While it is admirable to express this kindness to others, it is also important to care for ourselves. This symbol is a reminder to lighten up and lavish upon ourselves the same love and compassion as shown to others. Again, this is about balance.

Courage

Zibu translation: "Amali" (ah'-mah-lee)
Color: Black
Gemstone: Red Garnet
Physical Body: Back of Neck (Cervical spine) & Upper Back (Thoracic spine)

"Courage brings strength to the surface. It bridges the inside with the external. It manifests itself in action. It is directed by Spirit. It is connected with Spirit. Courage hears the Truth and understands the possibilities. It connects outcome with action. It allows a view of what is possible. Courage and Heart combine in strength. It is an unbeatable combination. It reaches goals. It reaches heights previously unknown. Courage brings Truth to the forefront."
—Blessings from the Angels

Many times, people are surprised at how much courage they have inside. It takes a special circumstance to bring the courage to the surface as a reminder of what is held inside.

One woman emailed me and explained that she had gone through a tough time in her relationship with her ex. She knew they were wrong for each other and that she deserved to be treated better. When she finally got in touch with the courage within, she felt strong enough to end the relationship and subsequently felt a huge weight lifted from her shoulders.

She was led to the Zibu website and found the Angelic symbol for Courage, which strongly resonated with her. This is the symbol she had tattooed on her wrist as a reminder to be fearless, as well as a reminder that the Angels are always with her and watch over her and protect her. Her last statement to me was, "Now I will always be reminded of the person that I can be."

Creativity

Zibu translation: "Imono" (ee-moh'-noh)
Color: Pink
Gemstone: Rose Quartz
Physical Body: Heart

"As you embrace this symbol for Creativity, know you are a conduit for Divine Expression. This process is magnificent when allowed to flow effortlessly. See the Beauty in surrendering preconceived ideas and allow something even more grand to emerge. Release your tight control over outcome and go with the flow to be present in the moment and take in all the Joy afforded you as you allow the Divine to be expressed. It can be an exquisite experience."
—*Blessings from the Angels*

When I read Dr. Wayne Dyer's 2004 book entitled *The Power of Intention: Learning to Co-create Your World Your Way,* I was intrigued as he described the Seven Faces of Intention. Beauty is one of them.

Dr. Dyer explains intention as "a force in the universe that allows the act of creation to take place."

I asked the Angels to show me symbols which represented each of the Seven Faces of Intention, and they are listed in the book alphabetically. They are:

1. Beauty
2. Creativity
3. Expansion
4. Kindness
5. Receptivity
6. Unconditional Love
7. Unlimited Abundance

The energy emitted from this combination of symbols is palpable. I drew them on beautiful paper, and they grace the wall of my sacred studio space, so that I can see them daily and bask in the energy as I co-create Zibu jewelry with the Angels.

Divine Essence

Zibu translation: "Imu" (ee'-moo)
Color: Cobalt Blue
Gemstone: Pearl
Physical Body: Chest

"This symbol reflects your Divine expression...your very core. Your true essence is that of purity and possibilities. It is a reminder to you that all things are possible. Know that you can cast off anything that keeps you from experiencing yourself as a true and pure expression of the Divine. All things are possible with this knowledge. There is nothing you cannot achieve. Whatever you embrace and believe, you can make your own. Rise to the occasion and step forward in confidence knowing you are limitless."

—Blessings from the Angels

This is one of the newest symbols shown to me by the Angels. During a recent reading for a friend of mine, a powerful and encouraging channeled message came through. I felt intense love-filled energy flow through me.

Throughout the reading, the Angels drew this symbol repeatedly right in front of my face. It was as though it was being drawn on a transparency that was superimposed on everything else. During the hour-long reading, I saw it drawn over and over.

The Angels showed me very clearly through images and physical sensations that this symbol for Divine Essence would provide great reassurance for the person for whom I was reading. I saw and felt the symbol in gold as a necklace placed over my heart. They did everything they could to impress upon me the importance of a necklace for my friend.

We followed their guidance, and this is the reply from my friend upon receipt of her Zibu necklace:

"I got my symbol and it took my breath away. Now every time I look at it I get chills so I don't consciously know what it is doing for me, but IT WORKS! I love it!"

Effortless Connection

Zibu translation: "Habukana" (hah-boo'-kah-nah)
Color: Purple
Gemstone: Amethyst
Physical Body: Crown Chakra

"Effortless Connection comes with realization that there is no separation. There is no separation of Being from Being, and no separation of Being from Spirit. All are one. The separation that is sometimes felt is truly an illusion intended to confuse. Separation is a misconception. Celebrate this moment in the knowledge that all is in Divine Right Order and that all are, indeed, connected. This realization is needed to break the mental image of isolation. Open your eyes to see your fellow expressions of Spirit."

—Blessings from the Angels

The experience that brought this symbol to me was a magical one. I was at a retreat on Whidbey Island in the Pacific Northwest for several days. South Whidbey is stunningly beautiful with lush green forested areas and plenty of wildlife. Much of our time was spent out in nature. At one point during the weekend, I was walking down a pathway in a wooded area and I could hear a chorale of Angels singing off in the distance. The area felt pure and sacred.

One of the assignments handed out that day was to go outside and ask Mother Earth for assistance with a specific issue. This was something new for me. I was guided to an extremely tall tree with an outcropping of long welcoming braches. I reverently knelt before this tree in quietude. When I was moved to ask my question, I sensed with my whole being that my request had been heard and had been honored. I checked in with my inner knowing, and knew this was correct. The instantaneous connection seemed effortless.

When I returned to the meeting room and my notebook, I was guided to draw this symbol and heard the words "Effortless Connection" which summed up my experience. This powerful image always comes to mind when I see the symbol.

Embrace

Zibu translation: "Anala" (ah-nah'-lah)
Color: Pink
Gemstone: Amethyst
Physical Body: Ribcage

"Embrace the richness of every moment in your life. No moment is meant to be wasted or missed. Be present in each moment to savor the Joy that abounds. Embrace it and make it your own. Joy is not to be merely observed. It is to be Embraced and absorbed and shared with others. A gentle, heartfelt Embrace with another is a beautiful way to deliver joy...from one Heart to another Heart. Do not underestimate the tremendous power of an Embrace. It is a glorious manner to elevate the experiences of one another. Be a conduit for Joy and pass it on."

—*Blessings from the Angels*

It has taken me many years to discover the benefits of hugs or embraces.

When I asked the Angels which part of the physical body was associated with the symbol for Embrace, I was happy to see "ribcage." It was a reminder that hugs or warm embraces between two people involves a connection at the ribcage, or chest, level. The heart resides in the left side of the chest wall, and when giving an embrace, it is especially effective when one heart can meet the other. This can be achieved by keeping your head to the right side of the person you hug, as placement of hearts is ideal.

As the Angels said above, "it is a glorious manner to elevate the experiences of one another." I share joy as often as I can by giving and receiving hugs, and always offer an embrace upon completion of an Angel reading for a client. It is a renewable resource, costs nothing, and is extremely valuable!

Embracing the Possibilities

Zibu translation: "Rimu" (ree'-moo)
Color: Orange
Gemstone: Rainbow Moonstone
Physical Body: Upper Arms

"You sit in the center of a spiral. As you look up, you can see there are multitudes of options. There once appeared to be no way out; however, now is a time to celebrate as you become aware of the glorious possibilities. What once appeared as tones of grey begins to take on a rainbow of colors. Each color brings with it many choices—each one more magnificent than the other. What initially appeared as a maze becomes increasingly more clear. It is a grand time to embrace the possibilities in your life and celebrate the unfolding mystery."
—Blessings from the Angels

This symbol celebrates possibilities, and I can see it used with great results in combination with the symbol for "Release Expectations." It is interesting that the gemstone for both symbols is the same—"moonstone." The symbols complement each other as they echo the message of opening up to endless possibilities available once self-imposed restrictions are released.

This is a beautiful reminder to release and let go and allow the Universe to provide for you in even grander ways than you can begin to imagine!

Encouragement

Zibu translation: "Awanda" (ah-wan'-dah)
Color: Pink
Gemstone: Moonstone
Physical Body: Lungs

"Encouragement resides with Love. It embraces with ease. It flows to others, and it returns as well. It lifts the Soul. It brightens the day. It comes from the Heart. It brings resolution. It combines wealth. It breathes Hope into Life. It brings inspiration. It offers connection. It joins humanity. It offers Hope and shares Love."

—*Blessings from the Angels*

Greeting cards have always been a passion of mine. For many years, I bought cards and would either keep them for inspiration or mail them off to friends to remind them of how important they are to me.

Now I make my own cards, and the symbol for encouragement is an ideal way to send energy from the Angels. Sometimes I choose to add the symbol to an existing card, or I will draw the symbol in pink marker or on pink paper to amplify the energy. It always warms my heart knowing that I can make a difference in the lives of others even with a simple gesture of mailing a card with kind words. I know it brings inspiration to others and brightens their days...and it always comes from my heart.

Zibu

Evolution

Zibu translation: "Anika" (ah-nee'-kah)
Color: Pink
Gemstone: Obsidian
Physical Body: Gastrointestinal System

"Evolution refers to the growth and expansion of the Soul. It expresses the eleva-tion of thoughts and actions. Evolution is desirable growth and expression. As one awakens to the Truth, evolution is taking place. Evolution allows hearing of the Truth and ability to take action to move forward and upward. It is a beauti-ful path. It is well-lit and inviting. It is a glorious journey."
—Blessings from the Angels

Onward and upward! The symbol for evolution is about personal growth.

I have never enjoyed the thought of things staying the same in a stagnant manner. I read as much as I can and am eager to learn more and awaken more fully to who I am. Even when personal growth has been painful, I have always known that I will come out of the situation as a more evolved Soul.

When I first saw this symbol and discovered it was called evolution, I was impressed that it resembled a fetus, which is the epitome of personal growth! Nevertheless, it is a symbol which signifies something worth celebrating, as we all continue on our personal life paths.

Expansion

Zibu translation: "Hatatami" (hah-tah-tah'-mee)
Color: Gold
Gemstone: Amber
Physical Body: Shoulders

"We invite you to be awake and aware, Dear One, to new opportunities and new ideas. Be open to experiences which will broaden your vision of the world you live in. You will find a richness opening up to you in return. Your positive thoughts will become your reality. Celebrate this power of expansion."

—Blessings from the Angels

One of the "Seven Faces of Intention." See chapter on Creativity for the complete list.

In re-reading Wayne Dyer's book, *The Power of Intention*, the meaning of Expansion becomes more clear. He points out how we can stay open to Divine guidance by identifying with Universal Mind, which is ever-expanding. This allows for intellectual, emotional and spiritual growth.

I see this symbol being used to great effect at the beginning of the day. What a lovely gift to give yourself as you set an intention to open up to be aware and awake to new ideas and opportunities for growth.

As I start each day, I draw the symbol for Gratitude in the air with my fingertips. It is a perfect way to use the energy of the symbol while I draw prayers with my hands.

Expansion can be used in the same manner. Call on the Angels as you draw the symbol for Expansion at the beginning of your day, or at the start of a new project. Give it a try and observe how the Universe conspires to assist you.

Faith

Zibu translation: "Anuba" (ah-noo'-bah)
Color: Yellow
Gemstone: Citrine
Physical Body: Chest

"Faith is an unending belief of the goodness and beauty in all experiences. It draws near the positive energy. It embraces all that is Divine. It is a closeness to the Creator. It is a belief so strong to unravel the negative beliefs. Faith is the password. It is the key to unlock the beauty of the future, as well as the present. Faith is a magnificent connection. It is pure and clean and true. It holds a richness of its own. Faith is the opening to the Light. Illuminate your life with faith. It is a beacon."

—*Blessings from the Angels*

The symbol for Faith often appears with the symbol for Trust during readings. ogether these give a clear message to believe that all things are possible.

When I take time to journal, I often find myself drawing these two symbols as I begin writing. I have also drawn these together as framed calligraphy pieces. As I look at them, I sense a whisper of encouragement from those in the Angelic Realm. It is a reminder to keep going and not give up. All things are possible with faith.

Fluidity
Zibu translation: "Awina" (ah-wee'-nah)
Color: Green
Gemstone: Peridot
Physical Body: Neck

"Fluidity has to do with rolling from the old situations into the new ones that lay ahead. Your willingness to be fluid and flow with ease to the new will serve you well. Let go of past disappointments and see the joy in the new. Fluidity is a beautiful quality. It leaves rigidity behind. It opens you up to new expressions. Fluidity is flexible. It flows with grace and ease. Let go of the sides of the river and immerse yourself in the middle. The energy of the river will sustain you and carry you to all things good. Let go of your tight grip in order to experience fluidity, and celebrate the fullness and richness of Life."

—Blessings from the Angels

This symbol appeared at a woman's request for a custom necklace. I enjoyed the way the message came through with repeating references to water flowing like a river. It created an interesting visual image.

This woman returned from a trip to the mountains in the beautiful Pacific Northwest and shared her story with me. She and her friend were taking in the scenery, when both of them felt compelled to take a dip in the icy cold mountain river. She was disappointed to discover later that her symbol for fluidity came apart from the neckchain and washed away in the river. We both laughed at the irony.

The Angels reassured me that this was a sign that her work with the first symbol was complete, and she was ready for a new symbol.

Forgiveness

Zibu translation: "Anka" (ahn'-kah)
Color: Blue
Gemstone: Turquoise
Physical Body: Chest

"Forgiveness comes from deep within the Heart. It releases and frees all of those involved. It cuts the ties and lets go. The freedom experienced is exquisite. It lightens the Heart and elevates the life experience. Forgiveness from one can touch many. It is a beautiful expression. It removes the wall and allows continuation of forward motion."

—Blessings from the Angels

One day as I was drawing the symbols randomly on paper, it occurred to me that the symbols for forgiveness and happiness were quite similar. The spiral at the bottom changes from curling to the left to moving forward to the right.

It makes me think that happiness can be created through true forgiveness. When unforgiveness weighs heavily on the heart, the load can be lightened when forgiveness is given.

Several times during readings, this symbol has shown up in conjunction with the symbol for Universal Love. I was guided to make earrings for a woman one time where one was Love and one was Forgiveness. The Angels reminded me that the two work together, and that Love opens the door for Forgiveness to happen. Once the door is open, many blessings can take place.

What a beautiful reminder that is!

Fortitude

Zibu translation: "Anona" (ah-noh'-nah)
Color: Red
Gemstone: Peridot
Physical Body: Stomach

"Fortitude is a driving force. It never gives up. It moves forward with grace and ease. It holds the vision clearly. Fortitude drives with forward momentum. It is endless. It continues in the face of uncertainty. It bridges gaps. It continues forward toward the goal...toward the Truth. Fortitude is a strength. It connects with belief. It ties the future to the present. It is a reminder of what is possible. It is grand. It is achievable."

—*Blessings from the Angels*

As with the symbol and message for Faith, this symbol for Fortitude is about continuing to move forward on one's life path. When I see this symbol, I sense a team of Angels cheering to keep going and not give up.

This symbol showed up when I asked how I could assist an artist friend of mine who was having a tough time. Several aspects of her life were presenting challenges for her. I received guidance to make a necklace of this symbol and surprise her with it. As we had been friends for many years and she had helped me on numerous occasions, I was ecstatic that my request for encouragement for her was so clearly answered.

It always warms my heart when I see her wearing this necklace, as I know the Angels are walking with her and providing gentle and loving guidance.

Freedom

Zibu translation: "Komida" (koh-mee'-dah)
Color: Purple
Gemstone: Clear Quartz
Physical Body: Arms

"Freedom involves all aspects. It has options. It tends to all things. Freedom speaks to all. Reach for it to make it yours. It whispers in mankind's ears. It must be louder. It creates connections. It is meant to be shared."
—Blessings from the Angels

Occasions come up frequently when people notice the Zibu jewelry I wear and then invite me to bring samples of my jewelry to their office for staff members to see. I am always honored to share these creations and accompanying stories.

One day I was invited to an art center to informally display my artwork for a group of employees. At the time, I packaged each necklace with the name of the symbol on the backside, to allow customers to respond to the energy of the symbol, rather than choosing the symbol by its name.

As I was carefully taking each piece out, an employee came up and zeroed in on one specific necklace. I could tell it spoke to her. She turned the package over to see the meaning of the symbol, and quickly remarked that she definitely wanted this one. She promptly unpackaged the necklace and put it on and smiled.

When I asked for the details of what just transpired, she informed me that she had set an intention earlier in the week with her pastor around the word "freedom." And, of course, the only piece she was guided to pick up was the necklace with the Angelic symbol for Freedom. That was clear confirmation for both of us.

Friendship

Zibu translation: "Tama" (tah'-mah)
Color: Blue
Gemstone: Sodalite
Physical Body: Hips

"Friendship is a unity of Souls. It is a connection and appreciation of one another. It blesses others to acknowledge the God expression in them. It brings with it many life lessons meant to elevate the human experience. Friendship blesses all involved parties. There is always good intention. Growth through friendship can be magnificent. Friendship is meant to be shared freely with Love. All are participants. It is not exclusive. It spreads Joy through thought and action. It enriches life experiences. It adds light to life."

—Blessings from the Angels

Quite often during the translation process, upon hearing what the symbol is called, I relax thinking to myself, "oh, I know what this one means." However, when the Angels tell me their definition of the word, I realize how limited my scope is. This is exactly what happened when I received the symbol for friendship.

It amused me that I thought this was an easy one, and that I thought I already knew how to describe friendship. Even now, when I re-read what the Angels brought me, I smile to myself. "It blesses others to acknowledge the God expression in them." That has much more depth to it than my limited human vision.

I was commissioned to create matching necklaces for two women who were best friends. They were delighted when they saw the symbol. It is interesting that the part of the physical body associated with this symbol is "hips" as these two women told me they were such good friends, they were practically "joined at the hips."

Grace

Zibu translation: "Anan" (ah-nan')
Color: Orange
Gemstone: Citrine
Physical Body: Mouth

"Grace begins with the Heart. It comes from deep within and colors all actions. Grace is gentleness of action. It rises above the other thoughts. It washes clean. It is authentic. It resides with Love and Beauty. Grace blesses all. It is easily shared. It can easily be given to others. Graces holds the mysteries of the future. It carries much strength. It unites."

—Blessings from the Angels

One of the first Zibu necklaces I created for myself was a long chain with a combination of nine symbols on it. I always enjoyed explaining the significance of the symbols to those who commented on it.

A couple years ago, I helped out at a local art center and chose to wear my favorite necklace to work one day. One of the other artists was intrigued by the fluid shapes, so I began to tell her the story.

She pointed out one symbol that she was especially drawn to. When I told her that it meant "Grace," she was surprised at the coincidence because her name, Ann, means "Grace" or "Graciousness."

She chose a second symbol explaining that it was a shape she recognized as one she had drawn many times since she was a child. It was also a shape she incorporated as a component in some of her own jewelry.

As I eagerly told her its meaning was "Unity," I saw shock on her face. She covered her open mouth, tears welled up in her eyes, and she slowly backed away from me. I knew that something significant had happened, so I reassured her and asked her what she was feeling.

She acknowledged that there was no way I could have known this, as most people know her as Ann, but her first name was actually Unity. Her name was Unity Ann! I always appreciate how the Angels provide me with such clear confirmation.

Gratitude

Zibu translation: "Anu" (ah'-noo)
Color: Golden Yellow
Gemstone: Citrine
Physical Body: Solar Plexus

"Living in a state of Gratitude has enormous benefits. When one is grateful and sees all events and experiences as Blessings meant to enrich life...one will notice many more Blessings arriving in a constant stream. This state of being glorifies the purity and beauty of Life. Gratitude is a Blessed state to view the world, as it shifts the focus away from the negative and magnifies the positive. Bask in your Blessings and give thanks."

—*Blessings from the Angels*

While I love all the Angelic symbols, this one is particularly dear to me. I see myself as a person who is surrounded by blessings, but was not always aware of them in the past.

One day when I was focusing on, and muttering to myself about, one tiny aspect of my life that was not going well, I felt the presence of the Angels. I was shown the symbol for gratitude, and I drew it out several times.

What I felt next was breathtaking. I could sense the tips of Angel wing feathers gently touching my cheek and urging me to change the direction of my focus slightly. It was a brilliant demonstration of the power of refocusing one's attention. It allowed me to release my fixation on an irritation. When I took time to look in another direction, I was much more aware of all that was joyous.

It was a beautiful reminder that what we focus our attention on is magnified. I consciously choose to focus on the positive by beginning each day drawing the Zibu symbol for gratitude three times in the air with my fingertips. It represents a prayer to set my intention for the day.

Happiness

Zibu translation: "Asani" (ah-sah'-nee)
Color: Yellow
Gemstone: Hematite
Physical Body: Arteries

"Happiness is through & through. It saturates the body. It radiates from the Heart. It is readily shared. Happiness heals. It sheds light. It connects mankind. It grows in the Heart. It glows with light. It shines for others. It can be shared. It leads the way. All can hear it."

—Blessings from the Angels

Happiness is a perfect symbol to use in setting an intention for a positive outlook on life. It can be drawn and placed in a prominent location to be seen throughout the day.

I have found it useful to have this symbol plus the symbol for Joy on my pillowcase. Sleeping on Angelic energy is exquisite. When I travel, my pillowcase is one of the first things I pack to ensure a good night's sleep and a positive outlook in the morning.

The very first time I slept on Angelic symbols was a memorable experience. Up until that night, I would usually sleep curled up in a ball with my blankets over my head. But the very first night that I slept on a Zibu pillowcase, I observed myself as a I relaxed into bed lying on my back with my arms out.

When I awoke, my first thought was of being gently cradled in the arms of the Angels. I felt like I had slept on clouds. My husband even commented on my changed sleeping behavior.

I still enjoy a good night's sleep, but have to admit that the first night's sleep was the most dramatically improved. Never before had I felt so safe and loved while sleeping.

Harmony

Zibu translation: "Onoko" (oh'-noh-koh)
Color: Blue
Gemstone: Lapis Lazuli
Physical Body: Shoulders

"Harmony is a beautiful balance in which all will benefit. When things flow effortlessly in alignment and with grace, Beauty can abound. No one is made less and no one rises above in superiority. All are equal and complement one another. Things are seamless as they fit together with ease as puzzle pieces. Visualize how all mankind can elevate this experience by living harmoniously as it was meant to be. Harmony is a key ingredient in bringing peace on Earth."
—Blessings from the Angels

This graceful symbol is ideal for a work space or in a home. I was guided to paint symbols above some of the doorways in my home. Harmony is one of the intentions I set for my household as I painted a series of symbols above the entrance to my home. I am certain it blesses my family, as well as our guests.

Healing

Zibu translation: "Akashawa" (ah-kah'-sha-wah)
Color: Blue
Gemstone: Fluorite
Physical Body: Blood

"The heart is pure for one who can heal. Healing is pure energy transferred from Spirit. It comes from within and can be shared with others. It is intended to be shared to help those in pain and in need. Columns of strength unite for this expression. This benefits the world. It is easily transported and costs nothing. It remains a mystery but will be unveiled soon. It is for everyone. Help one another. Kindness heals."

—*Blessings from the Angels*

The symbol for Healing is one I use on a regular basis, and I have experienced powerful results.

A dear friend of mine had undergone bilateral hip replacement surgeries, and yet when I saw her months after the final surgery, she was still limping and in discomfort. She was receptive to my offer for some energy work, so I called upon the Angels for assistance.

We sat facing each other, and she sat with her hands palms down on her lap. I was guided to use the Zibu symbol for healing and was shown where to draw it with my fingertips in the air above her upper thigh. I held my palm face down over her thigh, and closed my eyes to see the Angelic guidance more clearly. What I saw in my mind's eye astounded me, as images of little white light energy rapidly zipped up and down her thigh and around her hip joint repeatedly.

Upon completion of their work, I opened my eyes to see that my friend had raised her hands about 12 inches above her lap and had kept them there during the session. I reassured her that I was able to do energy work without her moving her hands out of the way. She explained that her hands moved up on their own as though they were pushed upwards from an intense amount of energy in her legs.

The last part of the Angelic message for my friend was that she would sleep like a baby after this treatment. I checked with her the next morning, and she had, indeed, slept soundly and woke up refreshed. The best part was that she felt an immediate improvement in her hip.

Healing Embrace

Zibu translation: "Amami" (ah-mah'-mee)
Color: White
Gemstone: Pearl
Physical Body: Hands

"Consider the immense healing power of extending an Embrace to one another. Connecting to another through the kindness of extending open arms in Peace and Unconditional Love has tremendous healing powers. It transfers the spark that ignites the Passion to live Life from a place of brightness and possibility. Do not underestimate the magnificence contained and shared in an Embrace. It costs nothing and can be shared with ease."

—Blessings from the Angels

A couple years ago, a friend approached me with concern about a young woman who had given birth to a premature baby. There was uncertainty about whether this sweet little baby would survive, and my friend asked me to call in the Angels.

When I returned to my studio and spent time with the Angels, I kept seeing this baby being held in the supportive and loving arms of the Angels. I saw this symbol drawn in my mind's eye and heard the words "Healing Embrace." When I asked what part of the physical body was associated with this symbol, I was not surprised to hear "hands."

I was guided to draw the symbol out on paper and they showed me the symbol being posted above where the baby was sleeping. The Angels were surrounding the baby with love and light, and supporting her with this healing embrace. The image filled me with assurance that this baby would be fine, and I relayed the encouragement to my friend. The baby did, indeed, survive and is now thriving beautifully.

Heart Song

Zibu translation: "Nakata" (nah'-kah-tah)
Color: Orange
Gemstone: Red Garnet
Physical Body: Diaphragm

"We invite you to allow your heart to truly sing its authentic song. We ask you to remove the walls you have so carefully constructed around your heart. What seemed to be a protective device has resulted in a barrier to keep your heart from flourishing and rising up to sing its song. It is time to release this self-imposed limitation. It has been a barrier for you. Step into your spotlight and prepare to sing your life's most beautiful song. You may be surprised at the beauty and love you will experience. Embrace this moment and sing your heart's song."
—Blessings from the Angels

"Don't die with your song still inside you." Each time I recall this adage I am reminded of the importance of finding one's passion and inspiration. When you are inspired, it is easy to express the magnificence you carry within. Living purposefully is how we follow our bliss and receive fulfillment in our actions.

So let go of any fear, as it is the only stumbling block that will keep you from singing your heart song. The world is waiting to hear the magnificent expression that only you can deliver!

Honesty

Zibu translation: "Kana" (kah'-nah)
Color: Green
Gemstone: Peridot
Physical Body: Throat

"Honesty begins with seeing the Truth within. There is much strength in Honesty. It has the potential to open many sealed doors. Honesty reaches to the depth of the Soul. Honesty remains a beautiful goal. At its center is Truth. That is the place from which to live."

—Blessings from the Angels

Sometimes clients aren't too pleased to see this symbol come up during their Angel reading. I've learned that most people assume that this indicates they are dishonest. This is not true. The message the Angels want to impart with this symbol is a reminder for people to be honest with themselves.

Once I share this interpretation, the recipient often nods in recognition. The messages that come forth in readings are rarely huge surprises, but rather gentle reminders of truths that we know deep in our hearts.

Hope

Zibu translation: "Rizu" (ree'-zoo)
Color: Blue
Gemstone: Blue Aventurine
Physical Body: Neck & Upper Shoulder

"Hope promotes well-being. It is a reminder to keep moving forward. Hope connects the Heart to the future. It draws forward. It is a forward movement. Hope gathers strength to carry forward. It allows the glimmer of light to shine bright. It illuminates the path. It leads the way."

—*Blessings from the Angels*

One of the visualizations I provide when teaching classes on uses for Zibu symbols is infusing Angelic energy into our planet. Hope is a great choice for this; however, other possibilities are symbols for World Peace, Unconditional Love, Joy or Happiness. All of the symbols have positive intentions, so any of them would be beneficial.

Visualization

◆ Sit comfortably, relax and breathe deeply.

◆ Pull down a column of Spirit's pure white light around you.

◆ Call on the Angels and ask that they surround that with a spiral of golden, sparkly Angelic energy.

◆ Hold out your non-dominant hand palm up.

◆ Visualize holding the essence of the planet (or neighborhood, building, person or animal) in the palm of your hand. Take time to clearly see the details.

◆ Surround it with Spirit's pure white light, like a cocoon.

◆ Wrap a coil of sparkly, golden Angelic light around it.

◆ Use two fingers in your dominant hand (the hand you write with) and draw the symbols above it, within it or around it, as you feel guided.

◆ Take your time and draw the symbols slowly and feel the energy as it flows through you.

◆ When you feel it is complete, give thanks to the Angels for assisting you.

Illumination

Zibu translation: "Adinata" (ah-dee-nah'-tah)
Color: White
Gemstone: Opal
Physical Body: Eyes

"Light a candle in the dark, Dear One. The Angels are nearby always. We can help only at your beckoning. We await your call to aid you to see the light. The light is available to brighten your path to allow you sure-footedness. Please ask us to walk with you. We have much to offer to ease the load. The amount of love we have for you is enormous. We can breathe freshness into your days and restful slumber at night. We long to assist you. You need but ask. Life can be glorious beyond your wildest imagination."

—*Blessings from the Angels*

As I travel to give lectures about Zibu, I am always open to hearing from others how they are inspired to express the symbols.

A woman in Portland, Oregon shared a lovely image with me of how she envisions receiving the symbols into her chakras. That led me to write this visualization.

Visualization

◆ Sit comfortably, relax and breathe deeply.

◆ Relax your shoulders and relax your jaw.

◆ Pull down a column of Spirit's pure white light around you.

◆ Call on the Angels and ask that they surround that with a spiral of golden, sparkly Angelic energy.

◆ Visualize your crown chakra (top of head) opening.

◆ See the Zibu symbol gently floating down from the Heavens into your body and residing in your heart chakra (chest area).

◆ Know that the symbol and its energetic properties will be accessible to flow out through your own actions and thoughts and words and will be amplified with loving Angelic energy.

◆ Give thanks to the Angels for their assistance.

Try it and see what you experience, or personalize it to make it your own ceremony.

Inner Peace
Zibu translation: "Risoma" (ree-soh'-mah)
Color: Black
Gemstone: Snowflake Obsidian
Physical Body: Ears

"Inner Peace is a quietude that resides throughout. It is accessible when slowing down to look inside. It patiently awaits discovery. The key is slowing down the frantic pace to savor the Tranquility. This allows for a quiet body and mind. Much more can be heard and understood when the internal chatter ceases. The gentle whispers of the Angels can then be clearly heard. Inner Peace leads to other personal discoveries that enrich Life."

—Blessings from the Angels

The messages I receive from the Angels are always gentle and kind, and at times I have to laugh as I hear interesting phrases or slang.

The Angels bring encouragement for us to slow down and find time for quietude. It is difficult to hear their whispers when our minds are racing with thoughts. Sometimes, I am shown what busy minds look like with rapidly moving energy zooming around inside a person's head. The phrase I hear and am asked to relay is something like "Please slow down and quiet your mind. We aren't able to reach you with our words when 'the line is busy'."

They know I smile when I hear the message phrased like that, so they have continued to use it when appropriate. I love the clear visual image this provides!

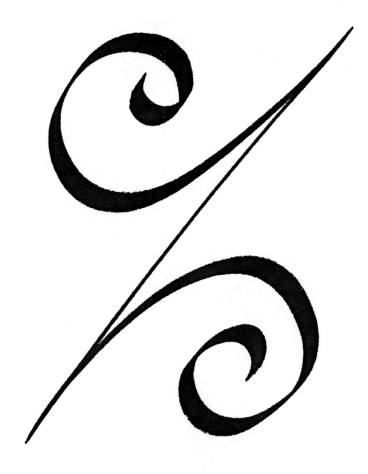

Integrity

Zibu translation: "Ikira" (ee-kee'-rah)
Color: Blue
Gemstone: Sodalite
Physical Body: Throat

"Integrity is a most admirable quality. Do not underestimate the power of consistently coming from a place of honesty and truthfulness. All pathways will be cleared of debris when one shines brightly in a place of integrity. Please notice how smooth the path becomes when one embraces truth and honesty. Interactions with others become almost effortless when this mindset is adhered to."
—Blessings from the Angels

When I first began to make Zibu jewelry in 2002, I was asked to make a custom necklace. I was guided to the symbol for Integrity which I made out of silver wire. The woman liked it, but was reserved in her response. I saw her months later in 2003 at a social function, and as we were talking, I noticed her Zibu symbol earrings. I thought they looked nice, but didn't remember making them for her. When I commented on them, she told me the rest of the story.

When she was getting dressed and ready to come to the social event that evening, she searched for some earrings to wear. At the back of her jewelry box, she found silver wire earrings she had purchased several years earlier from a department store. It wasn't until she put them on that she realized they were the exact same symbol I had channeled for her months earlier. That confirmed for her that this was the most optimal symbol for her to be wearing, and she now loves the necklace I made for her!

Joy

Zibu translation: "Anana" (ah-nah'-nah)
Color: Purple
Gemstone: Citrine
Physical Body: Solar Plexus

"Joy is the true essence of life. It is the core of all others. It brings with it richness and depth in life. It connects all to the Higher Power in true essence. Joy has depth and meaning on many levels. It combines Trust, Faith and Love. It is expansive. It is meant to be shared from the Heart. Joy is for all mankind to experience. It is here and available to all who seek it or ask for it."
—Blessings from the Angels

The details surrounding the day I received the symbol for Joy are crystal clear in my mind. It was on a Sunday afternoon, and I was driving home from church services. The pastor had shared an inspirational story around the theme of Joy.

As I reflected on the story on my drive home, I heard the quiet whispers of Angelic voices in my head. They had something they wanted to share with me about Joy. I wasn't prepared to write the message down, as I was driving my car, so I asked them to hold the message and deliver it to me later. They were insistent that it was important, so I found myself pulling off to the side of the road and scrambling to find a piece of paper and a pen.

This Angelic message was rapidly scrawled on the back of an empty Starbucks pastry bag, along with several versions of the symbol for Joy.

When I got home, I shared the story with my teenage daughter, who was quick to point out which version of the symbol was the correct one.

I love savoring the radiance I feel as I allow the Angels to speak through me, and it is just as joy-filled as I recall these special moments.

Kindness

Zibu translation: "Hazu" (hah'-zoo)
Color: Pink
Gemstone: Rose Quartz
Physical Body: Soles of the Feet

"Kindness is an action as well as a thought pattern. This type of action benefits many. The recipient of a kind gesture receives an energetic boost of life force which lingers long after receipt. The one expressing the kindness receives blessings from above for sharing unconditional love. Those viewing the act of kindness have their Hearts touched in a glorious way as the benefits are clearly demonstrated before them. Offer kindness freely to those around you...known and unknown...as all will reap great benefits."
—Blessings from the Angels

Kindness is one of the "Seven Faces of Intention" as covered in the chapter on Creativity. Please refer to that chapter for the complete list.

This is an excellent symbol to use when embellishing your work space. You do not need to permanently draw or paint the symbols on walls or furniture to bless an area. Energy can be infused into a work space, for instance, by drawing the symbols in the air and setting an intention.

In your own work space, symbols may be displayed tastefully in a frame on your wall or placed on your desk. See how clean and simple the Zibu symbols appear in a clear plastic frame. Trust and Faith are two others that would be excellent for a work area.

While visiting a young girl in a hospital a couple of years ago, I asked the Angels to bless her and infuse her with Spirit's healing energy. I also took time to draw Zibu symbols as I pointed to each of the four walls of her room, and the ceiling and the floor. The Angels told me that each and every doctor, nurse, caregiver, and visitor would be blessed as they came to see this special little girl.

It offers me so much reassurance knowing that I can make a difference by calling on the Angels to help others and teach others how to do the same.

Light Heartedness

Zibu translation: "Koha" (koh'-hah)
Color: Yellow
Gemstone: Clear Quartz
Physical Body: Feet

"Remember to look to the light and feel the lightness in your heart. Know that it will allow you to shine brightly for others. You have the potential to change the lives of others dramatically with this approach to life. It allows you to find lightness in your step, and by lightening up, you will be able to avoid taking things so seriously. It will also allow you to release dark stumbling blocks from your life's path."

—Blessings from the Angels

This symbol can be used at those times you find yourself having self doubts. It assists in fanning your internal flame of existence. It is a reminder of keeping hope and having faith.

In times of sadness or disappointment, reconnect with your Angels by drawing this symbol repeatedly. As you relax into the knowing that you are not alone, you will feel the heaviness lift and sense the brightness you thought was gone.

Listen Within

Zibu translation: "Rikomana" (ree-koh'-mah-nah)
Color: Light Blue
Gemstone: Blue Lace Agate
Physical Body: Inner Ear

"Please know that many answers reside within. Many Beings run frantically to search outside themselves to find the right answers. This action is disempowering. To settle in and fully accept one's personal power, it is important to find stillness and quietude. Constant action and noise mask the wealth of wisdom available to each and every Being. It is incredibly valuable to find quietude regularly to reconnect with the lifeline of Truth within. Take time to truly listen quietly. There is a wealth of information easily accessible when listening within."

—Blessings from the Angels

It is with interest that I have observed how people sometimes race from "expert" to "expert" to find answers. Others search for gurus to give them answers to life's mysteries.

While I do believe we can help one another, this is not meant to be a substitute for going within to hear our own truths and guidance. We all have the capacity to connect with Universal Consciousness, or God, or our Higher Selves, for the "wealth of information" the Angels refer to.

This book is written with the intention of assisting each of you in connecting with the Angelic Realm to receive your own answers. Zibu symbols are provided as a tool to assist you. They key is spending time to Listen Within.

Moderation

Zibu translation: "Nona" (noh'-nah)
Color: Green
Gemstone: Carnelian
Physical Body: Eyes

"Moderation is of key importance. It is the level to live at. It is a healthy level. It blends the two extremes. It meets in the middle. It is a key vantage point to see the whole picture. It is reasonable and realistic. It is at the core."
—*Blessings from the Angels*

Moderation is another issue I revisit on a regular basis. The Angels use this symbol as a reminder of the importance of blending two extremes to find balance in moderation. It is reasonable and realistic.

One evening in my studio, I was caught up in finishing several large orders for custom necklaces. It would have been beneficial for me to remember moderation and quit for the day, as it was getting to be late at night, and I had worked all day.

The Angels even told me several times that it was time to put my tools down and finish another day. But for some reason, I ignored the Angels and pushed on-ward. There was only one necklace left to create, and it required a 28 inch chain. It was late by now, and I was tired.

I only had 30 inches of chain left on the roll, so I quickly realized that I only had to cut off 2 inches for my 28 inch necklace.

Using the wire cutters, I snipped 2 inches off the length of chain, and some-how in my tiredness, I absent-mindedly folded the chain in half and cut it again! It only took a second.

I was so distraught realizing I had ruined the necklace and couldn't figure out how to fix my mistake. I clumped the three pieces of chain on my desk and went to bed. A day or two later, I finally felt able to face my studio again, but still unsure how to repair the damage.

The Angels brought me a miracle straight from God that day, as I discovered there were two pieces of chain on my desk—a 2 inch length and a 28 inch length. The chain had been repaired.

This was a powerful lesson for me about moderation and responding to An-gelic guidance. As a reminder, I now keep the 2 inch piece of chain pinned to the wall at eye level by my work table.

Again, I am grateful for the patience the Angels demonstrate over and over with me!

Nature
Zibu translation: "Kunata" (koo-nah'-tah)
Color: Green
Gemstone: Moss Agate
Physical Body: Hands

"The symbol for Nature is a lovely reminder of the precious gift of the planet. This exquisite gift is meant to be cherished and cared for...not destroyed for short-term goals. Find time each day to connect with Mother Earth and give thanks for her many treasures meant to sustain humankind. It is reciprocal in that humankind is asked to care for these precious resources. It is only offered once, and now is the time to honor the planet and show respect. Take time to connect with Mother Earth from a place of Gratitude and Awe."
—Blessings from the Angels

Before I met the woman who owns a metaphysical shop on Whidbey Island, we had talked briefly on the phone. Mutual friends had helped us to connect, knowing that we had information to assist each other.

After she heard me explain about Zibu and how I create jewelry in the shape of the symbols, she expressed an interest in knowing what the Angels had in store for her.

Prior to our meeting in person, I received guidance about her necklace, which included a symbol for Nature. The Angels expressed deep appreciation for her willingness to care for Mother Earth and her resources.

As I drove up to meet her and deliver the necklace, the first thing I noticed was the flourishing garden that welcomed guests to her shop. I smiled as I acknowledged the clear message about Nature that I had received earlier.

This was more meaningful as I got to know her better and discovered that she lives in a magnificent house made of all recycled materials. I thought that the symbol for Nature was a sweet way for the Angels to provide an introduction to my new friend.

Nurture

Zibu translation: "Ani" (ah-nee')
Color: Golden Yellow
Gemstone: Citrine
Physical Body: Head and Neck

"To nurture is to give loving attention to assist in growth and expansion. Hold the essence of your being in your loving arms and nourish yourself with positive and uplifting thoughts. Delving into the negative is a destructive habit. It is not conducive to forward motion and growth. It is a much more enriching pattern to shower oneself with unconditional love and watch all aspects come together in magnificence. There is no limit to what is possible when nurturing with loving energy."

—Blessings from the Angels

Similarities exist between the symbols for nurture and unity. They are similar in shape. The message of unity is an embracing and coming together of various aspects of ourselves...internal and external, thought and action.

I see this graceful symbol for nurture as an image that reminds each of us to embrace ourselves and recognize the precious nature of our being.

Order out of Chaos

Zibu translation: "Tatama" (tah'-tah-mah)
Color: White
Gemstone: Clear Quartz
Physical Body: Spinal Cord

"See the accumulation of random sparks of energy. When the lower vibrations reside with you, there will be experiences of confusion. A disharmony of energy creates an imbalance which will make for an unstable situation. Your navigation through this energy will slow your progress and hamper your ability to see clearly. Releasing the lower vibrational energy will lighten your space, which will have a profound effect on your surroundings and on you. Release and let go in order to bring in more Divine light and savor the serenity and balance."
—Blessings from the Angels

This symbol came to me in response to a request to help a client with improving the energy in his apartment.

He had a Feng Shui consultant come in and give advice on rearranging furniture and adjusting placement of household items in order to clear the energy in his place.

In addition to those changes, the Feng Shui consultant asked if I had an Angelic symbol to further assist the client. The symbol arrived quickly, and I enjoyed seeing what it looked like.

The spiral line represented disorderly chaotic energy, and the parallel lines showed me how the chaos would be transmuted into orderly and calm energy.

I drew the symbol on paper and instructed the client to place it under his front door mat. Each time he enters his residence, he will reactivate the calming orderly energy.

I was so moved by the energy in this symbol that I began using it in my home and studio, with great results.

Passageway

Zibu translation: "Akina" (ah-kee'-nah)
Color: Red
Gemstone: Bloodstone
Physical Body: Legs

"The Passageway is a threshold through which to walk. It is a symbol to represent acknowledgement of more than meets the eye. Walking through the Passageway is akin to going into a portal. This allows for travel to other ideas. It is an opening to opportunities and ways of thinking. When one feels stuck, it is beneficial to see the symbol for Passageway and mentally walk through to see new options not yet entertained. It is a portal to opportunities. Be awake and aware, and see the possibilities."

—Blessings from the Angels

Angelic messages routinely come through with a series of visuals for me. When I see the symbol for Passageway, it sometimes appears as an actual archway over a path. When I see a person's life path, I am literally shown a path in nature.

It is exciting to see this kind of image, as it indicates an opportunity to step forward and entertain new ideas. It is a nudge from the Angels to pay attention to "be awake and aware and see the possibilities."

Passion

Zibu translation: "Nokori" (noh-koh'-ree)
Color: Red
Gemstone: Moonstone
Physical Body: Lungs

"Passion is about balance. It is about expression. Expressing one's Heart. It stems from Beauty. They reside in the same place in the Soul. Passion is a strength. It ties the Heart to its goal. It is a connection. It is with us always—either dormant or active. It reflects our intention and our Soul. It connects us to one another. It brings warmth and joy. Awaken the Passion."
—Blessings from the Angels

The symbol for Passion was in the initial group that I translated. In those earlier days of learning to decipher the meanings, there was a sharp learning curve.

I laugh when I recall the circumstances around a request for a symbol for a mother's 14-year-old son. I was apprehensive when the symbol for Passion appeared for this young boy. My ego was horrified that I would (mistakenly) appear to be advocating the type of passion portrayed on the cover of romance novels.

The kind and encouraging message from the Angels then came forth and dispelled my fears. They clarified the meaning of Passion as a connection from one's heart to its goal. I see it as a forward pull to keep us moving on our life paths. In times like this, I clearly see how I can get in my own way and am reminded to trust and have faith that I am receiving accurate information. This is an incredibly rich learning process for me.

Patience

Zibu translation: "Anoko" (Ah-noh'-koh)
Color: Yellow
Gemstone: Clear Quartz
Physical Body: Shoulder Joint

"Patience comes from being in the moment. Much can be learned by slowing down to be present and in the moment. It serves many purposes. It releases attachments to outcomes and expectations. Slow down and take in all the information. It is not always as it seems. Patience comes from the Heart and remembers Love."

—*Blessings from the Angels*

There are times when I lose my patience. I try my best to slow down and allow things to unfold in their own time, but I do have my moments when I can't seem to find my patience. In these instances, my teenage daughter has been known to saunter in front of me with my first Zibu booklet opened up to the symbol for patience and mischievously ask if I know this symbol and if I have read the meaning of it lately. She is very subtle at times.

The most beneficial way that I use this symbol is to draw it on the back of my left hand with a black permanent marker. As I draw the symbol, I ask the Angels to infuse me with the essence of patience. I could use my finger to draw the symbol, and it would be just as effective; however, I choose to use a marker. This acts as a visual cue for me throughout the day.

Another story that comes to mind about patience happened one evening as I was preparing to give a talk to a local group about Zibu. I went from table to table chatting and getting to know the audience beforehand.

I was carrying a few copies of my original booklet of symbols, when one older woman impatiently asked me to explain what in the world I was going to talk about. I began telling her about the symbols and how they were brought to me by the Angels. I quickly flipped open the booklet to show her an example, and it fell open to the symbol for patience, the symbol relating to the shoulder joint.

The impatient woman was stunned as she read the information, and related to me that the reason she was wearing an arm sling strapped tightly to her body, was to immobilize her injured shoulder joint. After the synchronicity of seeing the symbol for patience and its relationship to the shoulder joint, she quickly settled down and expressed eagerness to hear my lecture.

Peacekeeper

Zibu translation: "Hana" (hah'-nah)
Color: Pale Blue
Gemstone: Clear Quartz
Physical Body: Pectoral Muscles (Chest)

"This symbol represents a role that is assumed. This has a gentleness to it and yet strength. It is a gentle power. This role is key in demonstrating the power of cohesiveness in finding peace. One in this role reminds others of options not entertained previously. Peace is the way is the message. Mankind requires reminding. The message bears repeating. Mankind requires a constant reminder from ones who are Peacekeepers. They hold the lantern of Hope for the survival of mankind."

—Blessings from the Angels

Peacekeeper is the symbol I was shown during a reading for myself. It was when I was just learning how to hear the information.

This symbol kept coming up for me, and I knew it had significance, but it took me a while to figure it out. I came to find out it was being used as a title of sorts and that it reflected part of my life's purpose.

My husband knew how much this particular symbol meant to me, so as a gift on my 50th birthday, he gave me a silk blouse that had been hand-painted with this symbol on the back. I can think of no other gift I received that year that meant as much to me as that one. It is a one-of-a-kind creation that feels exquisite when I wear it.

I heard the Angels whisper "Don't worry...we've got your back covered." They must know how much I enjoy a sense of humor!

Persistence

Zibu translation: "Atu" (ah'-too)
Color: Orange
Gemstone: Citrine
Physical Body: Skeletal System

"Persistence connects the Heart with its goal. It is a reminder to keep moving forward in search of answers. It is a beautiful strength. It demonstrates to others the power of believing and trusting the outcome. It is a forward drive for answers. This energy comes from Spirit. It is an undeniable forward pull. It is a magnetic pull to the Truth. All answers can be found in the Truth. The Truth is all that is needed."

—Blessings from the Angels

Up until this point, I have focused on symbols used in the home or work space. Please know that they can also be used in your car.

One client who received the symbol for Persistence asked me if it was okay to hang it from the rear view mirror in his car. He explained that he spends much of his time driving and wanted that Angelic energy with him. I reassured him that the symbols can be used virtually anywhere and encouraged him to give it a try.

As more people feel the inspiration to incorporate the symbols into their lives, the possibilities for uses will multiply. Listen to your own guidance and see what comes forth for you.

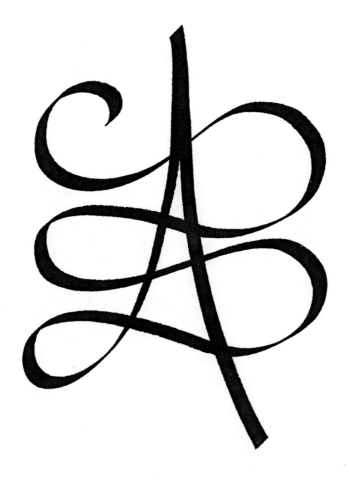

Prosperity

Zibu translation: "Ana" (ah'-nah)
Color: Green
Gemstone: Peridot
Physical Body: Small Intestines

"Prosperity begins within. It refers to richness and abundance. It has to do with acknowledging the Beauty within. Prosperity opens the doors for good to arrive in its fullness. Prosperity is a richness within. It is available to all who ask. Reach out to connect with your prosperity. It fills the Heart. It radiates to others. It is to be shared freely with others. It has a fullness and richness to it. It has depth to it. Share the prosperity."

—Blessings from the Angels

Many people express interest in the symbol for Prosperity with a financial goal in mind. In re-reading the Angelic interpretation, it is clear that it is also a reference to a richness within.

It has to do with expressing kindness and gratitude. As they say, it fills the heart and radiates to others.

When someone claims to live a rich life, they often are expressing gratitude for the precious gifts in their lives, such as their health, their family and their friends. How true!

Purity

Zibu translation: "Ama" (ah'-mah)
Color: Yellow
Gemstone: Moonstone
Physical Body: Genitalia

"Purity is clarity. A clearness to see past the flaws to the Truth. It is a clean slate. A fresh beginning. It is a smooth surface. Purity shines brightly in those who believe. It is place to return to in order to understand. It brings with it Angelic connection. Purity allows for growth in a beautiful way. It opens the door for brightness and illumination. All shines clearly."
                                                    —Blessings from the Angels

My husband was eager to try out one of my first experiments with symbols drawn on a pillowcase. The Angels guided me on the specific combination to assist him. Purity was one of the many that were included.

Upon awakening the next morning, he was ecstatic about what transpired for him. He is an extremely creative person and loves color, so I was stunned to learn that up until that night, he had only dreamed in grey tones.

He reported that all of his senses had been awakened while resting his head on the Angelic energy. As he reflected on his dreams, he was keenly aware of the vivid colors, the sweet fragrances, and clear stereophonic sounds. He had no idea that dreams could feel so rich.

Each person's experience sleeping on symbols will be unique to them. Earlier in this book, I told of my own experience with my first pillowcase. My dreams have always been extremely colorful, so my experience was personal by bringing me a level of comfort and security I had not had felt before.

Receptivity

Zibu translation: "Matanu" (mah'-tah-noo)
Color: Red
Gemstone: Coral
Physical Body: Heart

"Receptivity has to do with removing personal blocks in order to receive all that is available to elevate the human experience. When blocks are cleared, then the doors are open to receive information to assist with elevation. Old belief patterns can block the receptivity without full knowledge of the reason for lack of information. A humble and sincere request for removal of any and all blocks renders them useless. The gateways are open to allow a flood of Divine messages to flow forth. A state of Receptivity is a blessed place to reside."
　　　　　　　　　　　　　　　　　　　　　—Blessings from the Angels

Many of these Angelic symbols appear to express their meaning in their shapes. This one clearly shows me the feeling of reaching up with both hands to the Heavens in a position ready to receive. The spirals give me the impression of opening one's hands.

I recall an experience years ago when I was baffled at my apparent inability to receive. As I explained this to my friend, I flung my arms out exclaiming, "I'm ready to receive...why is it not happening?"

However, when I glanced out at my hands, I was horrified and embarrassed to see them clutched tightly into fists. My lesson was about opening my arms and hands to receive after asking the Universe to provide. It seemed obvious after the fact, but it bears repeating. Ask and it shall be given; however, one must be open and willing to receive.

Reciprocity

Zibu translation: "Takima" (tah'-kee-mah)
Color: Green
Gemstone: Jade
Physical Body: Hips

"What flows in for one is meant to be shared. It is a delicious Balance to receive and then give to others. The energy is continuous when allowed to flow through rather than being hoarded. Blessings which arrive for one are meant to be shared freely with others. Nothing is meant to be hoarded. All is intended to be shared with compassion and kindness to one another. One need not suffer as another is elevated. All are encouraged to share their blessings."

—*Blessings from the Angels*

A client requested a custom Zibu piece for her partner, and this symbol was shown to me by the Angels. When I delivered the piece along with the channeled message, my client realized that Reciprocity was the component missing in her relationship with him. She had been struggling to make the relationship work, but came to face the fact that she was the giver and her partner was the taker. She told me later that he was unwilling to make changes to keep a balance of give and take, and they ended up going their own ways.

Again, the Angels were not delivering new information, but rather were confirming what she already knew to be true in her heart.

Reconnection

Zibu translation: "Rimi" (ree'-mee)
Color: White
Gemstone: Labradorite
Physical Body: Shoulders

"This symbol represents reconnecting to Source. When one is unplugged, one is disconnected from the life-sustaining energy. Vitality can be embraced again when connecting to Spirit and recognizing all are one, and there is no separation. Any separation one may feel is an illusion and is a result their own action of pulling their own plug. To reconnect again is as easy as visualizing placing one's plug into the Universal outlet. This image combined with the sincere request to receive life-affirming energy from Source will resume the constant flow of glowing white light."

—Blessings from the Angels

A mother contacted me for a symbol for her young son. He has a lot of energy that always seemed to escalate at bedtime. That was the most challenging time of the day for the parents. The boy fought every aspect of getting ready for bed.

The symbol for Reconnection showed up for him, but the format was in wire suspended by a blue ribbon. The guidance was to hang it above his bedroom door, and I saw it gently emitting sweet energy to assist this young boy in reconnecting with himself.

His mother called me the day after the symbol was placed in his room. She was thrilled to report an immediate reaction to the energy shift. At bedtime, he quietly toddled out and took his mother by the hand and asked to be put into bed. He was very calm and went to bed without a fuss.

An additional aspect to this story is that the mother had recently gotten a Zibu Angelic symbol necklace, and I believe that the child was also responding to her shift in energy.

Reflection

Zibu translation: "Anini" (ah-nee'-nee)
Color: Green
Gemstone: Ametrine
Physical Body: Mouth

"This Angelic symbol for Reflection is a beautiful reminder of your role to reflect the Divine. The actions you take and the words you speak reflect your inner being. Take time to reflect before doing or saying to see if it is consistent with your authentic self. Let your expression be a true and accurate reflection of who you are. As you communicate clearly, know that what you receive in exchange is more clear communication from others. It will be apparent that you come from a place of sheer Joy and Delight as you clearly reflect your Divinity."
—Blessings from the Angels

Much of the Angelic message for Reflection has to do with reflecting outwardly what resides within. It is another reminder about the importance of authenticity.

The image of this symbol is a clear representation of Reflection, as it is a mirror-imaged symbol. The right side is a reflection of the left side.

This symbol is an ideal one to use in combination with Sacred Place and Tranquility as you prepare to meditate. Consider drawing these three symbols and placing them on your altar as a subtle reminder. Another option is drawing the symbol in your palms to cradle the energy in your hands as you relax into a meditative state.

These are my suggestions to give you some ideas, but I encourage you to follow your own guidance to see what fits your needs best. You will intuitively know!

Release

Zibu translation: "Rakuna" (rah'-koo-nah)
Color: Blue
Gemstone: Chalcedony
Physical Body: Arms

"The symbol for release is a reminder to let go of the stumbling blocks in your life. The blocks that keep you from moving forward with Grace and Ease are obstacles you hold onto. The belief pattern that one must struggle keeps one tied tightly to illusions of blockage. Taking time regularly to Release old beliefs that no longer serve you optimally will assist you greatly as you stride forward on your life path. Release and release again to keep a clean slate and allow effortless movement forward. Release and let go of those beliefs that hold you back from experiencing life to its fullest."

—*Blessings from the Angels*

The symbol for Release is one I use on a regular basis. It is significant that the place I am guided to draw the symbol is on the palm of the hands. I regularly carry with me a black permanent marker. It works beautifully as a visual reminder of setting an intention to release and let go.

For more information, refer to the section at the back of the book on "How to Use the Symbols." There are specific steps detailed on releasing fear and doubt, or other stumbling blocks.

Release Expectations

Zibu translation: "Atuna" (ah'-too-nah)
Color: White
Gemstone: Moonstone
Physical Body: Solar Plexus

"We encourage you to release expectations to release the screening device in place. This screening restricts the abundance of what can come forward for you. By releasing expectations, you open yourself up to endless possibilities. You will be surprised and delighted at the beauty and perfection of responses to your requests when you allow Spirit to provide for you in full. By removing your filtering system and implied restrictions, you will allow the Universe to provide for you in perfection.

—Blessings from the Angels

It seems that people usually don't have a problem asking the Universe, or God, or Spirit, for what they desire. However, it appears that we sometimes like to also dictate specifically how we want our answers to be delivered.

This Angelic message brings with it a reminder to release the details of how our prayers are answered. We limit ourselves when we believe the answers can come only in one form. Ask, and then release expectations, to experience the fullness of receiving.

Resilience

Zibu translation: "Inoko" (ee'-noh-koh)
Color: Golden Yellow
Gemstone: Pyrite
Physical Body: Shoulder Blades

"Resilience goes hand-in-hand with hope. We remind you to not give up hope. Hope gives life meaning and connects you with something greater than yourself—as with faith. Faith is a belief so strong as to release fear associated with negativity. We surround you with Spirit's pure white light as we encircle you every minute of every day. You are never alone."
—Blessings from the Angels

The Angels remind us to not give up hope. When faced with difficult situations, the key to resilience is keeping faith and hope.

I have found that the overall theme of all the Angelic symbols is hope, love and encouragement. It is obvious to me that Zibu symbols convey these reassurances even without written messages. Many people have been brought to tears from touching or viewing the images.

One of the very first deliveries I made was to a client who appeared to be silent as she gazed down at her new necklace. I kept waiting for her to respond verbally and nothing was happening. As I was standing and she as sitting, I had to lean over to see her eye-to-eye. I was shocked to discover tears flowing down her face. I hadn't learned yet how powerful the energy was in these Angelic symbols.

Years later, I am not concerned when I see tears, but rather relieved, as I know the Angels have deeply touched the person's heart.

Right Action

Zibu translation: "Ontu" (on'-too)
Color: Cobalt Blue
Gemstone: Lapiz
Physical Body: Hands

"Right Action is at the core of your movements right now. You may doubt at times, but the forward movement you are experiencing is optimal for you. It is not without difficulty, but the personal growth will be tremendous. You are more than strong enough to face the issues ahead with this symbol as a reminder. You move forward like never before, and you do so with grace and ease."
—Blessings from the Angels

I have shared this story many times during lectures, and I always recall how perfectly everything unfolded.

A local woman requested that I create a custom Zibu piece for her daughter. She made a brief reference to the fact that they were in the midst of a legal situation.

The symbol for Right Action showed up, and I was guided to make a hand-held meditation piece. Once I finish a custom piece, I usually feel an urgency to get the piece to the recipient, which was the case with this one.

The mom worked close to where I live, so I decided to hop in the car and make the delivery. I would normally make a phone call ahead of time, but chose to follow my instincts and just drive there unannounced.

I arrived at the office just in time to see her putting on her coat in preparation to leave and pick up her daughter. Unbeknownst to me, they had an appointment with the attorney. She was scheduled to give her testimony or deposition. I was delighted to know that I responded to the nudge from the Angels for a timely delivery of the piece.

The mom called me the next day to thank me for the Zibu symbol, and she put her daughter on the phone to explain. The daughter expressed her initial anxiety and uncertainty about going ahead with the case, but when she read the message and felt the Angelic energy, she was convinced she was taking the Right Action.

She kept the wire symbol in her pocket during the proceedings. She told me that each time she felt herself beginning to cry or emotionally lose control, she would feel her pocket warm up.

The Angels provided reassurance and comfort through this gesture. She said that this happened several times exactly the same way and gave her the strength to finish answering the attorney's questions.

I never know the exact details of how the Angels plan to help others through the Zibu symbols, but it is always perfection...and I'm always filled with gratitude to be a conduit through which this energy flows.

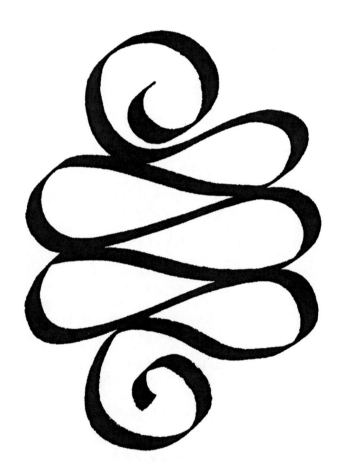

Risk

Zibu translation: "Anuki" (ah-noo'-kee)
Color: Black
Gemstone: Onyx
Physical body: Muscles

"Risk stepping into the spotlight to be seen and heard. You have precious gifts to share with mankind. Please step forward to express yourself so all may hear. Express this gift to others and enrich your life and the lives of those around you. You can make a tremendous difference."

—*Blessings from the Angels*

At times when uncertainty creeps in, it is beneficial to take time to meditate on the symbol for Risk.

As always, the energy is very gentle, and I usually end up feeling a gentle push to step forward and share what I've been thinking. Each person is unique with beautiful gifts meant to be shared with the rest of mankind.

This is a lovely reminder to each of us, that we have special talents and wisdom, and have the ability to make a huge difference in the world. Each person plays an important role, as we assist one another.

So when trepidation sets in, remember to find an internal place of quietude and reflect upon this symbol to recall the importance of taking the risk to be seen and heard.

Sacred Place

Zibu translation: "Shikawa" (shee-kah'-wah)
Color: Purple
Gemstone: Rose Quartz
Physical Body: Top of Head (Crown Chakra)

"This is a reminder that each person holds a sacred place on this Earth Plane. It is meant to share with others. All that is needed is Heart. The world will follow this lead. Bring together what we need. We can help one another to hold this Truth. It is what we are here about."

—Blessings from the Angels

As I mentioned earlier, I have a studio where I co-create jewelry with the Angels. I consider it my sacred space, and treat it as such. The music I play in that room is carefully selected and sculptures of Angels are perched on almost every flat surface. I keep a cluster of colorful flowers in a ceramic vase handmade by my daughter. It is also the room where I meditate.

Before making any jewelry, I always take time to call upon the Angels to come in close and be with me. I ask that they hold my hands and bless my tools and materials. When the pieces are completed, I always ask that they be blessed. If the piece is for a specific person, I hold the image or name of the person with me while creating the piece, and ask that it be blessed specifically for them afterwards.

My studio is a very special place to me, and I know it is reflected in the energy. I have designated this as my sacred place to work by drawing the symbol above the door. I was taught at an early age to not draw on the walls in our home, so I have to admit that there was something very satisfying about pulling up a chair and standing on it while drawing the symbol in huge permanent marker on the wall of my studio as an adult.

I have two cats that are sensitive to the energy in my home. One of them loves to join me as I work. She gets so eager to go into the studio, that once I let her in, she immediately falls to the floor and rubs her face in the carpet and rolls around frantically and meows a special sound I only hear in my studio. That alone is confirmation for me that this holds palpable magical energy.

Sacred Union

Zibu translation: "Abu" (ah'-boo)
Color: Purple
Gemstone: Amethyst
Physical Body: Third Eye Chakra

"In the quietest of moments, one can look within and see the reflection of the Divine. The connection is always there when one stops to look and listen. In that moment, perfection can be observed. This symbol is a reminder of the undeniable connection. The spark of light that is the Divine is the invisible common denominator."

—Blessings from the Angels

At some of the larger metaphysical expos where I have had a booth, I have displayed a banner of symbols painted in gold on a colorful background as my signage.

The first day I used my new banner, I was intrigued when person after person would stand just outside the perimeter of my booth staring at the symbols. It was interesting that their facial expressions looked remarkably similar. Each person had a perplexed look and glazed over eyes. I had never experienced this before at the previous events.

Finally, as I began to bring them into conversation, I heard the same comments over and over. Each person would remark on how "the symbols looked familiar somehow." It was uncanny that they used nearly the same phrase each time. It was as though the symbols were allowing them to access some long-lost internal information.

What I enjoyed most was the second day of this two-day event. Again, I saw this same behavior as people would stop and stare at the banners. This gave me the opportunity to greet them and say, "They look familiar somehow, don't they?" It was wonderful to see such rapid positive responses.

What I received later was that each person was recognizing the symbols on a soul level, which I find fascinating. I know that more will be revealed from the Angelic Realm, as the time is right.

Self Care

Zibu translation: "Kinota" (kee-noh'-tah)
Color: Green
Gemstone: Turquoise
Physical Body: Gastro-intestinal System

"Each soul is entrusted with a physical container. It is a sacred temple to be cared for with the utmost of reverence and love. Caring for this vessel and keeping it filled to capacity with light is essential. Darkness and issues of struggle are to be released to keep a shining light. It is this light that illuminates the life path."

—Blessings from the Angels

This lovely symbol shows up regularly during readings for other Lightworkers. For those who feel a strong need to help mankind and see their life purpose on a grand scale, it is especially important to take time to care for ourselves. This is a key ingredient in keeping ourselves healthy and centered, so we can continue to give out of fullness rather than depletion and emptiness.

As I mentioned earlier, people who are givers may not always remember to share the same gifts with themselves. This symbol, which is a variation of a heart or Love, is a perfect one to draw out on paper and post in various places in your home as constant whispers to keep you on track to eat in a healthful manner, to get fresh air and exercise regularly, and to get plenty of rest.

Self Knowledge

Zibu translation: "Aki" (ah'-kee)
Color: Black
Gemstone: Tourmaline
Physical Body: Musculo-Skeletal System

"We encourage you to slow down and remember to take time to look within. Many search for answers outside of themselves, when the answers all reside within. Please see yourself as the vast source of all wisdom. It is carefully housed within and is accessible upon inner reflection. Do not doubt the connection, for it is always available to you. Quietude and reflection are the keys."
—Blessings from the Angels

Self Knowledge is the message that came through for a friend who does energy work. I knew she had a series of challenges before her, but was not aware of the details. Once I forwarded the Angelic advice, she ordered a necklace, bracelet and earrings featuring this symbol. She immersed herself in her quest for information about who she is and what her life purpose is. She was on the path to discovering her authentic self.

Our lives got busy, and we lost touch with each other for a while. I recently heard from her and understood the soul searching she had done. I learned that upon much reflection, she has found clear answers about necessary changes in her marriage, her day job and her energy work. She went on a meaningful trip to Tibet, divorced her husband to live on her own for the very first time in her life, and received certification in a yoga program that brings her much joy.

I saw her recently, and she was radiating such a bright light and looked happier than she had in years. Changes are not always comfortable or easy, but when it is in preparation for living more authentically, it is divine and is readily visible to others.

Serenity

Zibu translation: "Adu" (ah'-doo)
Color: Yellow
Gemstone: Amethyst
Physical Body: Ears

"Serenity calms the Heart to hear the messages clearly. It opens the doors and windows to the mind to know the answers. It holds the magic. All is as it should be when Serenity is experienced. It brings together the whole being. It embraces all. It carries the answers and leads to Truth. It is a Blessing. Open your arms to receive it."

—Blessings from the Angels

Symbols can be used in specific combinations to further set an intention. After reading the Angelic message above, see how well Serenity would work with the symbols for Centeredness, Listen Within and Tranquility. The main focus is about slowing down and finding quietude to listen to the internal messages, which will bring about an experience of Serenity and Tranquility.

As you start to notice themes with various symbols, consider using them in combinations as you are guided. The possibilities are limitless!

Simplify

Zibu translation: "Ki" (kee)
Color: Light Blue
Gemstone: Chalcedony
Physical Body: Toes

"Simplify the complexities of your life. The true meaning and purpose of life is often times clouded by the busy-ness and constant movement. These actions only serve as distractions to keep one from seeing clearly. One cannot see when life is lived in a fast pace with no room for reflection. The outer world is a reflection of what is going on within. To understand more clearly, slow down to look inside and feel the quietude. Your hearing and knowingness will be greatly enhanced by this simplification."

—Blessings from the Angels

The main message with this symbol is about slowing down for quietude and introspection, which echoes messages of other symbols. However, when I see this symbol during Angel readings, sometimes the theme is about trying too hard to force a specific result.

What I hear is "Stop making it so complicated. It can be much easier than you imagine." Usually my client will quickly realize exactly what the Angels are referring to. I don't need to give them details, as they are already aware of this internal struggle. As I have said earlier, these Angelic messages serve as reminders of what the clients already know in their hearts.

Soul Reintegration

Zibu translation: "Ritan" (ree-tan')
Color: Dark Blue
Gemstone: Lapis Lazuli
Physical Body: Spinal Cord

"Soul reintegration has to do with coming back to the original blueprint for living. When a life is lived in an in-authentic manner, fractures in the soul occur. The incongruities continue and cause difficulties and challenges until one takes time to come back to center and accurately see what their life purpose is. When one is on track and living authentically without compromise, the soul can reintegrate and become a full accurate reflection of the person with their soul shining brightly."

—Blessings from the Angels

When traumas are experienced in our lives, fractures in our soul occur as parts split off. This symbol can assist in setting an intention and asking the Angels for help in bringing all parts back for reintegration.

I do a lot of my writing on the computer and am responsible for its maintenance to keep it running smoothly. There is one program that I run when the computer starts to function less than optimally. It is the defragmentation program.

The Soul Reintegration symbol reminds me of the defrag program, as it provides reorganization and streamlining. As the Angels explained above, this will assist the person's soul to shine brightly.

Call on the Angels with this symbol and see how they can guide you to get back on track and live authentically.

Synthesis

Zibu translation: "Kalu" (kah'-loo)
Color: Lavender
Gemstone: Clear Quartz
Physical Body: Face

"Synthesis is a combining of all aspects of one's life. It is a layering and fusing of each portion of an individual. It is an integration of all facets. When separation or segmenting occurs, the whole picture cannot be seen. Relationships are elusive and life feels fragmented. A re-uniting of all aspects of one's life brings details into fine focus. This is where life lessons are connected and combined. Synthesize and bring it together."

—Blessings from the Angels

One interpretation of this message has to do with the theme of authenticity and change. It refers to incorporating who you were with who you are becoming. It can be a loving process of blending the old and the new into a something entirely different. Synthesis can be a beautiful process of melding into a new composition.

I was not surprised when I noticed the symbol resembles two hearts coming together side by side and connecting in the middle. I'm not always aware of the significance of the image when I initially draw the symbols, but it is much more clear upon reflection at a later point.

Tandem Connection

Zibu translation: "Hasu" (hah'-soo)
Color: Green
Gemstone: Jade
Physical Body: Eyes

"Tandem Connection illustrates two parallel worlds. They are side by side and are connected. You act as a bridge between the two worlds offering hope and encouragement. Your role is a pivotal one. You are here to offer your abilities to help mankind with much love in your heart. By giving to others, you fill your own cup. This symbol represents much more than what can be seen visually. It holds many other messages that will be revealed with time."

—Blessings from the Angels

Several years ago I heard a speaker from Australia at a Seattle metaphysical bookstore. She was extremely kind and compassionate, and I sensed such a bright light about her. She is a medium whose lecture was about her experiences connecting clients with their loved ones who had crossed over.

I was so impressed by this beautiful person that when I went for my own reading the following week, I gifted her a Zibu symbol necklace. The symbol I was shown for her was Tandem Connection. Once again, the shape of the symbol clearly expresses the message of the two worlds being connected by a bridge.

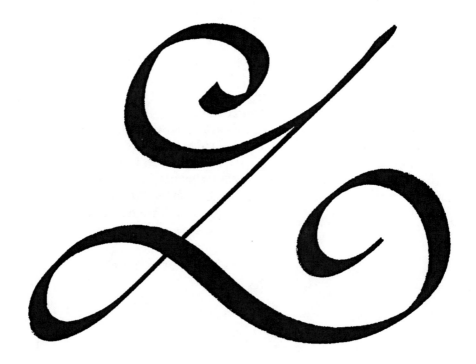

Thrive

Zibu translation: "Tina" (tee'-nah)
Color: Green
Gemstone: Jasper
Physical Body: Ribcage

"To thrive is to live life in rich awareness of all the beauty and blessings. It is self-perpetuating as energy is released and blesses those around. This way of living illuminates the areas within and around the person. It is an abundance that comes from within and can easily be shared and not diminished or depleted in the process. To thrive is to celebrate life in the present moment without fear of future uncertainties. It is a strong centeredness surrounded by gratitude."
—*Blessings from the Angels*

A client asked to see the Zibu symbol for Thrive. Up until her request, I had not seen the symbol before, but when it appeared, we both agreed it was perfect. I ended up creating earrings as a birthday gift for her partner, who I believe is the epitome of someone who lives in rich awareness of all the beauty and blessings which surround her. I also see her as someone who experiences life from a place of gratitude.

Our paths cross periodically, and she is almost always wearing those earrings. I sense that they are providing daily encouragement to celebrate her life in the present moment and to let go of future uncertainties. I can just imagine the Angels whispering sweet words, urging her to continue to thrive.

Tranquility

Zibu translation: "Mómina" (moh-mee'-nah)
Color: Purple
Gemstone: Carnelian
Physical Body: Back of Neck and Arms

"Tranquility is an oasis. It hears all and nothing at the same time. Becoming tranquil is essential to opening your Heart to hear. It calms the mind to listen for the Truth. Tranquility sheds light where it is dark. It cannot be rushed or forced. It flows when it is allowed to. It washes the Soul and refreshes. It has no needs. It just is."

—Blessings from the Angels

Tranquility will always be one of my favorite symbols, as it was the very first symbol I translated. As I mentioned earlier, I began drawing pages of symbols before knowing what they meant. After the Angel visited me during the Reiki treatment, I knew I was to receive messages about the symbols.

When I attempted this the first time, my eyes scanned the page of 50 symbols, and I asked the Angels which one I was to learn about that day. There was one symbol that had a whitish glow around it and seemed to rise up from the paper. I pointed to it and asked if that was the one. I got a clear yes.

I asked the Angels what it meant, and I quieted my mind. As clear as a bell, I heard only one word…"tranquility." Since I was being asked to be a messenger, I asked what they wanted me to share with mankind, and they provided the message through automatic writing.

It began very slowly at first, and the process has streamlined since that time. The Angels have been immeasurably patient with me as they have taught me this routine of relaying information.

Transition

Zibu translation: "Sokana" (soh'-kah-nah)
Color: Green
Gemstone: Aquamarine
Physical Body: Cellular Structure

"Transition is not to be feared. When it is embraced and welcomed, it brings with it much wonderment. When transition or change is deflected, the doors of opportunity close. Staying in one place is not a desirous plan. It is limiting the scope of one's experiences. To fully embrace life, one can open up to changes and take delight in the gifts and blessings that appear. Step forward in certainty knowing your life is enriched beyond your immediate knowledge with transition."

—Blessings from the Angels

I have to admit that I'm perplexed when I meet people who proudly claim they have not changed in years. It is a difficult concept for me to embrace that a person would desire to remain exactly the same.

This Angelic message celebrates Transition or change. It is a great reminder to embrace life fully and observe the gifts that appear. Sometimes the blessings can be seen more clearly retrospectively.

It makes me think of when I was pregnant with my daughter and was preparing for her imminent birth and had just begun my maternity leave from an office job. My husband came home to tell me he had been laid off from his job. This felt like the worst possible time for a change like this.

What I discovered later was that this was a magnificent blessing, as I had delivery complications and was confined to bed for a couple of weeks. He was at home and available to care for me and our newborn daughter. When the crisis was over, he quickly found employment again.

So in the midst of transition, it was initially very unsettling, but afterwards, it was clear that all was in Divine Right Order!

Trust

Zibu translation: "Tamana" (tah-mah'-nah)
Color: Green
Gemstone: Amber
Physical Body: Larynx / Voice Box

"Trust opens the doors for possibilities. It releases the blocks and allows for inward movement of Love. All those who experience Trust are available to experience even greater things. Trust is an opening of a sealed door. Open up to the possibilities."

—*Blessings from the Angels*

At one point in writing this book, I got wrapped up in my finished product and began to slip out of the present and venture into the future by way of fear. Uncertainty crept in as I wondered how I could possibly complete this project.

What began from the pristine place of being led by Spirit switched over to a place of Ego, as I found myself experiencing doubt. This forced me to stop and take notice of what was occurring. I sat up straight at my desk and took several deep breaths. Each time my lungs filled with oxygen, I felt my shoulders relax. It gave me enough time to see the framed symbols on the wall. It was the combination of Faith and Trust side by side.

As my eyes lingered on these symbols, I was reminded that all is well and to trust the process. It only takes a split second to reconnect with Spirit with non-verbal reminders from the Angels with their symbols. I felt my Ego step aside as I settled back into the comfortable role of co-creating this book with the Angels.

Truth

Zibu translation: "Hamani" (hah-mah'-nee)
Color: Blue
Gemstone: Hematite
Physical Body: Forehead (Third Eye)

"Truth resides in us all. We all have access to it. Align with Truth to understand. It offers explanations for everything. Truth connects from the Universe to the Heart. The Heart receives the Truth. Truth is to be shared with others as it is revealed. Truth equals Divine Right Order. It is the answer. It eliminates Fear. Truth encompasses all."

—Blessings from the Angels

During my initial phase of learning about Angels and receiving Heavenly guidance, I was taught how to use a pendulum. This proved extremely helpful in verifying the information I was receiving.

When I was prompted to create my own pendulums, the one symbol that shone brightly for me was the one for Truth. As one holds a pendulum and asks for a response to questions, the request is for truth. This is the only symbol I use when making pendulums, as it is a perfect match.

Unconditional Love

Zibu translation: "Reko" (ree-koh')
Color: Opalescent
Gemstone: Diamond
Physical Body: Complete Physical Structure

"Unconditional Love parallels Divine Love. It is pure and has no agendas or attachments. There are no expectations and no judgments. It is clear and transparent as Spirit's pure white light. It is to be offered to all and denied to none. The richness of the act of loving unconditionally is a cornerstone of living as Spirit deems most holy."

—Blessings from the Angels

Initially, I was shown the symbol for Universal Love. When I was asked what the symbol for Unconditional Love looked like, I wasn't surprised at what came through.

The shape of a heart with two spirals was clear. It appeared with two parallel lines or what looked like an equal sign superimposed on the heart, and three dots on the side. The image was stunning; however, when I received the message about Unconditional Love paralleling or equaling Divine love, the parallel lines made more sense to me.

When dots appear with Zibu symbols, they always appear in threes. The power of the number of three is unmistakable as representing the trinity in various religions. It can also represent past, present and future; birth, life and death; or body, mind and spirit.

So this symbol tells a story in its image. It clearly represents Unconditional Love paralleling Divine love.

Unity

Zibu translation: "Tatano" (tah'-tah-no)
Color: White
Gemstone: Clear Quartz
Physical Body: Lower Back

"Unity is a combining of all aspect of yourself. It is bringing them all together. It is the ability to let you see yourself as you truly are. Unity is a connection. It unites parts within you, but also unites or connects you with others. It combines and brings all elements to your Heart—the center of your being. It is where it gathers. It is where it blends together. It is essential for your being. Combining and uniting your aspects will make you stronger. It will make your voice stronger. It will allow you to carry all the messages simultaneously."
                                        —Blessings from the Angels

It is surprising to me how often the image of the symbol actually resembles the meaning of the symbol, or even the image of the associated body part.

The idea of Unity is about bringing together or uniting. As I reflect on the image, it appears like a face and two arms embracing something on either side and bringing them in together.

This concept rang true when I was asked by a woman to create a necklace for her mother, who was undergoing treatment for breast cancer. Unity is the symbol that came through loud and clear with a message about the importance of the members of the family coming together in support. I saw the woman in the center, and it was her arms that were embracing and uniting her family through her strength and courage.

Universal Love
Zibu translation: "Ziwa" (zee'-wah)
Color: Orange
Gemstone: Citrine
Physical Body: Heart

"Universal Love commands attention. It is needed to bridge the gaps. It is needed to unite mankind. It draws us together in strength. It is waiting to be shared freely without holding back. Universal Love radiates warmth. It touches the Soul. It frees the Mind. Share it freely."

—*Blessings from the Angels*

A friend of mine lives in Hawaii and is an accomplished artist who is well-versed in numerology, astrology and a variety of types of energy work.

On her visit to Seattle, she spent some time with me, and I shared with her my first booklet of Zibu symbols. It was still very new to me at this point. While I was enthusiastically relating to her my exciting experiences with this new method of working with the Angels, I noticed that she was flipping the booklet open and closed repeatedly.

I finally had to stop mid-sentence and ask her what she was doing. She smiled and said she was listening to the energy of the symbols. It sounded like nature to her.

I was thrilled to hear her say that, as I, too, could hear the energy of this language—though it sounded like brush strokes on canvas or a smooth vibrational version of Morse Code. Up until this point, I had hesitated to tell anyone I could hear the symbols, as it seemed a bit too far out there, even for me.

It is important to tell you that when my friend saw the symbol for Universal Love, she reminded me that she channels Universal Heart Energy and the logo she had created for herself was a rainbow of colors superimposed on this same symbol—a heart with a spiral on the right side.

Heaven just continues to verify my experiences and encourages me forward on this marvelous journey.

Unlimited Abundance

Zibu translation: "Lahika" (lah-hee'-kah)
Color: Brown
Gemstone: Amber
Physical Body: Hips

"Unlimited Abundance has no end and knows no boundaries or limits. It comes to those who ask in sincerity and have clear purpose in mind. When the pathways are cleared of debris, the natural flow of Abundance can run freely. Unlimited Abundance is the natural order of Life. It is as Life was meant to be."
—Blessings from the Angels

As a gift for a friend, I made a special pillowcase with the symbol for Unlimited Abundance. This amazing person gives generously of herself to others on a regular basis, and I wanted to create something special to assist her.

She routinely sleeps on this pillow and has told me many times of the love and comfort it brings her. What I've observed is her marked increase in ability to manifest abundance in her life. It is a joy to witness.

In the message above, the Angels point out the importance of having a clear purpose in mind. It is also about intention, as it is crucial to monitor your thoughts while setting an intention for abundance. More will show up for you, but you want to be clear about what you want to show up.

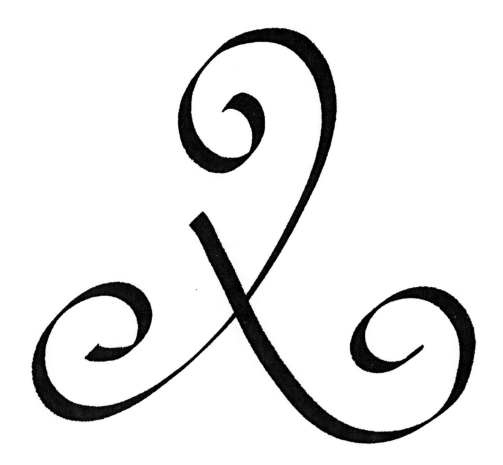

Vitality
Zibu translation: "Hamada" (hah-mah'-dah)
Color: Orange
Gemstone: Carnelian
Physical Body: Lymphatic System

"Vitality is a richness of the Soul. It resides with Passion. Both are needed together. It makes many things possible. It enables magnificent things to happen. Vitality serves a great purpose. It moves us forward. It keeps us in the flow. It works with the other symbols in combination. It brings things close to the Heart. It adds dimension to life. Vitality is Angelic connection with the Soul. It is expression. It is of utmost importance."
—*Blessings from the Angels*

The symbol for Vitality is one of my favorites to infuse life-enhancing energy into food and beverages.

Consider the value in taking time to bless your meal with this symbol. As I prepare meals in the kitchen, I like to add the special ingredient of Angelic energy. It doesn't take long at all. I merely hold my hand palm down over the food and visualize the symbol, or draw the symbol above the food with my fingertips.

It has also worked well to paint this particular symbol on drinking glasses.

Whether the symbol is visible or not, when the intention is set, the Angels respond.

Willingness

Zibu translation: "Tatina" (tah-tee-nah')
Color: Red-Orange
Gemstone: Ruby
Physical Body: Soles of Feet

"Willingness is a place of humility when one is ready to take action as directed from within. This is a place of pureness as one steps forward knowing all is in Divine Right Order. It is a place without doubt and fear. It is a place from which to spring forward. Willingness brings with it great opportunities for growth and insight. It is not without challenges, but brings great benefits and blessings. It opens the door for greatness to come forth."

—Blessings from the Angels

One of my Lightworker friends requested a Zibu piece for her 10-year-old son. She felt strongly that this was something that would assist him. I had not met him before, so it was a pleasure to check in and see what the Angels had in mind for this young boy.

A loving message came through along with this symbol for Willingness. I created a hand-held meditation piece with a wire-wrapped stone and a wire expression of the symbol.

When it was completed, I was invited to her home to give it to him personally rather than mail it. She intuited, and I confirmed, that it was a key component to his receiving special gifts from the Angels. This young boy was a delight with an abundance of energy. He eagerly opened the package and read the message and held out his Zibu piece. He surprised himself, as well as us, as he blurted out "This represents everything I have done in my life...and everything I will do in my life." He stopped abruptly and asked us, "What did I just say?"

His mother later told me that she discovered him crying while sitting in the kitchen after I'd left. When she questioned him, he explained how strongly he felt the presence of God during our interaction. It was clear that a special connection had been reopened between the Heavens and this boy.

Wisdom

Zibu translation: "Azula" (ah-zoo'-lah)
Color: Purple
Gemstone: Fluorite
Physical Body: Crown Chakra

"Wisdom can be tapped into by any who ask. Please know it can be accessed by anyone. Recall how close this is to you and how easily it can be reached. As you relax into your knowing, see that all is available to you when the veils are removed. Nothing is withheld from you. It is the blocks of your own creation that impede your progress. Slip into that space of knowing without any doubt whatsoever that all is available to you with grace and ease."
—*Blessings from the Angels*

My daughter has always acted as a very old soul, so it was no surprise that the symbol that came up for her was Wisdom.

When she was born, I was under the impression that I was here to raise her and share with her the knowledge that I have. At age three, she was pointing out the blessings that are all around us and how important it is that we are grateful for them. That is when I had a clue that she may have something to teach me.

I tell her daily how blessed I am to have her as my daughter. As time passed and after hearing me say this over and over, she finally told me, "Mom, you do know, don't you, that I chose you and Dad as my parents before I was born?" Now it is absolutely clear to me that she is a precious gift loaned to us from Spirit, and I listen to what she is here to teach me.

World Peace

Zibu translation: "Amin" (ah'-mihn)
Color: Blue
Gemstone: Clear Quartz
Physical Body: Nervous System

"It represents a peaceful and calm time in the world. It is a time people look for-ward to. People will work together to make it happen. People need to cooperate. They need to love one another. Peaceful times are ahead if we hold this vision. The world can be a safe and harmonious place for all of mankind. It is as it is meant to be. There can be much love and understanding in the world. It holds the hope for the future. Mankind can benefit from working together to make it happen. It is all we have to work with."

—Blessings from the Angels

This is one of the first symbols that I deciphered with the help of the Angels. It also has brought some interesting stories to me about how people's lives have been positively affected.

At one of the local metaphysical events a couple of years ago, a woman bought a necklace from me with the symbol for World Peace. She loved the idea that the associated gemstone was clear quartz, as she had a clear quartz sphere at home that represented our planet. Her intention was to lovingly place the Zibu symbol on top of her quartz to allow it to spread its energy 24 hours a day. I was touched by this kind gesture and see the image clearly in my mind each time this symbol comes up.

The other experience occurred when I went to Portland, Oregon to give a class on Zibu and its uses. I demonstrated how to infuse the planet with healing energy. I invited the group to participate as I led a visualization of holding the es-sence of our planet in the palm of one hand and using fingertips of the other hand to draw symbols above or within it.

When I got back to Seattle, I had an email from one of the students who shared with me his personal experience using the symbols. This very dear man detailed how he had been inspired to dance the symbols when he got home from class. He visualized holding the world in his hand and infusing healing energy. He suddenly sensed the strong presence of an angel and was deeply moved. He wrote the following poem to capture the essence of his experience.

Angel Dance

I danced with an angel
We held the world
We blessed all creation

Moving in joyful stillness
We laughed
I cried

Each tear wed the world
In holy matrimony
Divine being with Divine being

In the end
In the beginning
We simply kissed

The whole world was made new!

The poet is Norman Mitchell-Babbitt, and I thank him for allowing me to share this precious poem.

The walls of my studio are covered with artwork created by friends and each piece holds special meaning to me. The poem is matted and framed and is a central piece hanging at eye-level as a loving reminder of the rich experiences brought to us by the Angels.

How to Use the Symbols

These Angelic symbols can be used in any number of ways, but the following are offered as suggestions. I invite you to check with your own inner knowing as to how the symbols can best assist you.

Please keep in mind the importance of inviting the Angels in beforehand in whatever way you choose and finishing by giving sincere thanks.

Wear or Hold the Symbols

My initial contact with the Angel during the Reiki session in 2002 revealed the guidance for me to recreate the symbols as jewelry. Again and again, they have reminded me that these symbols are most effective when a person either "holds" or "beholds" them:

◆ To actually have physical contact with the symbol in some concrete form, such as wearing a necklace or earrings or holding a meditation piece; or

◆ To view or see as visual reminders, such as a matted or framed calligraphy symbol.

Here are but a few of the many benefits of wearing or holding these powerful Zibu symbols:

◆ Enhances alignment with Guardian Angels
◆ Provides stability in times of distress
◆ Brings comfort and clarity when feeling discouraged
◆ Assists in balancing energies that promote health
◆ Helps your Heart to remember your Divine purpose on this earth plane
◆ Provides encouragement in moving forward in the most optimal way on life path
◆ Harmonizes the auric field

Draw on Your Body

The act of drawing symbols on your body is a magnificent way to infuse Angelic energy. This also acts as a visual reminder of what is occurring.

My favorite place to draw symbols is on the back of my left hand. I am right-handed, and will often draw a symbol in black marker as a visual cue of the Angelic assistance I am requesting.

At times when I feel out-of-balance, I will select the Zibu symbol for "Centeredness" to adorn the back of my hand.

Try it with any of the symbols you are inspired to use.

Release Fear and Doubt

The Zibu symbol for "Release" is a great one to draw to release any number of things that do not serve us well.

Fear and doubt are two stumbling blocks that many people struggle with. The symbol for "Release" can be used very effectively by drawing it in the palm of your hands, rather than on top of it, as it represents opening your hands to the Heavens and letting go.

After drawing the symbols, visualize filling your hands with all your fears and doubts. I find it effective to actually exhale as I see my hands fill with a black misty cloud of the thoughts and feelings I want to release. Then raise your palms to the Heavens and invite Archangel Michael to remove them and transmute them into light. This can be repeated as many times as necessary. Finish by expressing gratitude.

Please know that even though the ink may wash off, the energy is still present.

Embellish Your Home

There are many places within your home that Zibu symbols can be used. Look around and consider your many options. In my own home, I have symbols painted on my coffee table, my lampshade, on the walls in our meditation room, on the wall in my studio, and on our front door.

Another effective place to paint Zibu symbols is above doorways to bless those who walk under them. It is a soft whisper of Angelic energy, which continues to gently shower sparkles of Angelic light.

There are many symbols to choose from; however, consider the value of painting the symbols for "Harmony" or "Creativity." Choose whatever resonates with you.

Energize Your Work Space

You do not need to permanently draw or paint the symbols on wall or furniture to bless an area. Energy can be infused into a work space, for instance, by drawing the symbols in the air and setting an intention. Symbols may also be displayed tastefully in a frame on your wall or placed on your desk.

"Receptivity" or "Kindness" would greatly enhance any work area!

Sleep on Angelic Energy

It is also very effective to sleep on Zibu symbols. Your choice of symbols can be drawn on a piece of paper and placed under your pillow, or may be drawn on your pillowcase with fabric markers.

Imagine the comforting feeling of sleeping on the energy of "Thrive" or "Clarity of Purpose."

Mail Blessings to Others

Bless those to whom you send mail...either correspondence, or better yet, when paying bills.

When I pay bills, I draw the symbol for "Blessings" where the stamp goes and then take a moment to visualize sending blessings to the recipient. I then cover it with a postage stamp to seal it.

Another option is to draw symbols on checks...such as "Blessings" or "Unconditional Love." I have noticed that customers are beginning to use symbols on the checks they mail to me!

Set an Intention with Your Checkbook

As many people strive to become prosperous and receive abundance in their lives, I invite you to consider the benefits of infusing your checkbook with symbols.

I personally have chosen to draw the symbols for "Unlimited Abundance" and "Prosperity" on my checkbook cover. For added assistance, I have drawn the symbol for "Balance."

Symbols Purify Water and Food

Masaru Emoto writes about how "words purify water" in his series of books on "Messages from Water." He has photographed crystal formations in water, and how it is affected by words and pictures.

He has clearly shown how water can be purified and blessed with words. Therefore, water and fluids can also be purified with Angelic symbols. As the average adult human body is comprised of approximately 70% water, it is compelling evidence to place your attention on the quality of water you consume.

Experiment by drawing symbols on paper to use as a coaster or tape the symbols on a cup or glass. This is a beautiful way to infuse Angelic healing energy into water or liquids you drink. The water you bathe in can also be blessed with Angelic symbols.

The same thing can be done with food before eating. Hold your palm over your food and ask that the Angels infuse healing energy, or vitality, or whatever you choose. See that symbol in your mind's eye. You may also draw the symbols in the air over your food with your fingers (I use my first two fingers).

"Choose Life" is a powerful energy to infuse into that which you consume.

Unconditional Love to Strangers

Send Unconditional Love to strangers. This can be done with or without their knowledge, and is a wonderful way to share Angelic energy. As I am driving and see panhandlers standing with their cardboard signs asking for money, I choose to send them blessings.

Visualize drawing in your mind's eye one of the Zibu symbols on a person's Heart Chakra, such as "Unconditional Love" or "Blessings."

Infusing Angelic Energy into the Planet

One more beautiful way to express these symbols is to hold the essence of the planet in your hand and draw healing symbols around it, above it, or within it. I often choose "Unconditional Love," or "Kindness," or "Beacon of Hope."

I guide students in my classes to do this in unison at the completion of my talk, and it feels great to come together as one and bless our precious planet.

Express Gratitude with Symbols

Begin the day with Gratitude. It is a beautiful way to focus on the positive in your life. Focus on the positive and give thanks...and more blessings will arrive.

I have been guided by the Angels to give thanks as I begin each day with a ceremony of drawing the symbol for "Gratitude" three times. It is a special way to say a prayer with graceful hand movements...like prayers in the air!

And so it is that I finish this book expressing gratitude to those of you who have been inspired to read these loving messages from the Angels. I feel honored to have been part of this magnificent process. Blessings.

Tables of Zibu Symbols and Translations

The next pages feature tables summarizing the Zibu symbols discussed in this book. The translation of the symbols appears on the following pages. It is an ideal format with which to use your pendulum or inner knowing to identify the most optimal symbol to assist you at any time.

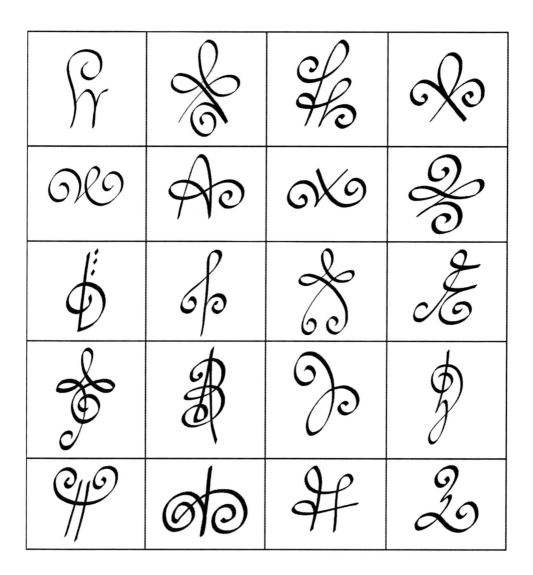

Abundance	Acceptance of Optimum Health	Authenticity	Awakening
Balance	Beacon of Hope	Beauty	Begin Anew
Blessings	Buoyancy	Celebration	Centeredness
Choose Life	Clarity of Purpose	Compassion	Courage
Creativity	Divine Essence	Effortless Connection	Embrace

Zibu

210

Embracing the Possibilities	Encouragement	Evolution	Expansion
Faith	Fluidity	Forgiveness	Fortitude
Freedom	Friendship	Grace	Gratitude
Happiness	Harmony	Healing	Healing Embrace
Heart Song	Honesty	Hope	Illumination

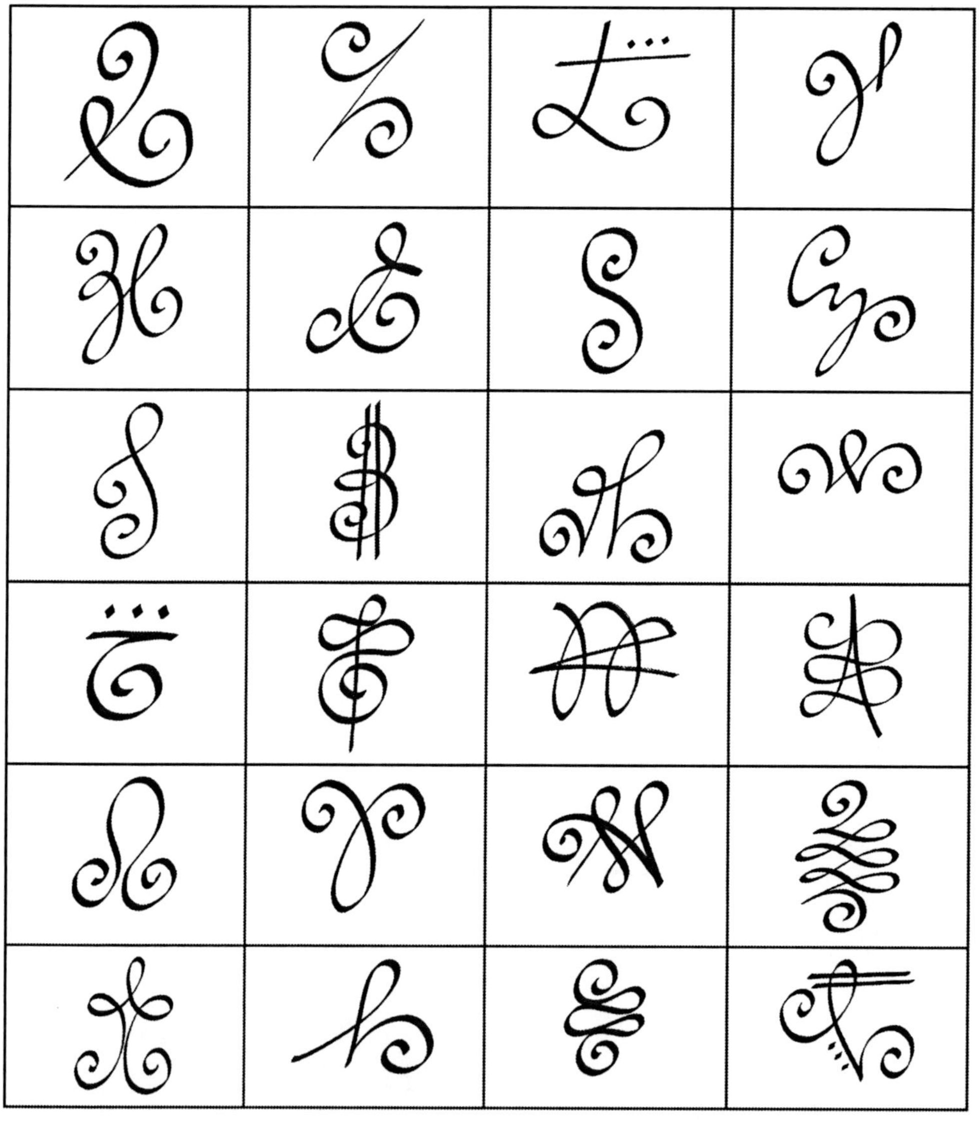

Inner Peace	Integrity	Joy	Kindness
Light Heartedness	Listen Within	Moderation	Nature
Nurture	Order out of Chaos	Passageway	Passion
Patience	Peacekeeper	Persistence	Prosperity
Purity	Receptivity	Reciprocity	Reconnection
Reflection	Release	Release Expectations	Resilience

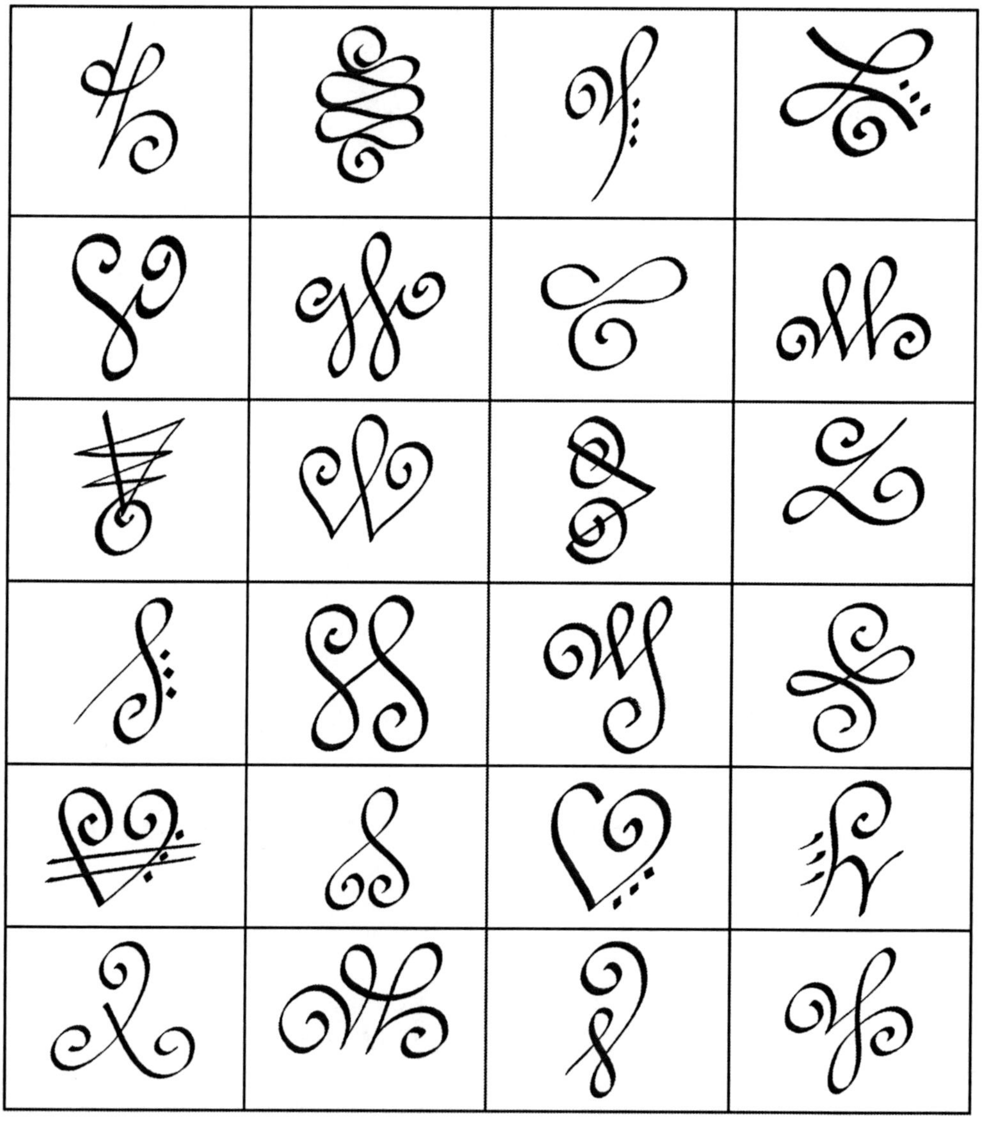

Right Action	Risk	Sacred Place	Sacred Union
Self Care	Self Knowledge	Serenity	Simplify
Soul Reintegration	Synthesis	Tandem Connection	Thrive
Tranquility	Transition	Trust	Truth
Unconditional Love	Unity	Universal Love	Unlimited Abundance
Vitality	Willingness	Wisdom	World Peace

About the Author

Debbie Zylstra Almstedt is a Seattle artist who has been channeling graceful symbols and inspirational messages from the Angels since 2002.

In October 2006, Debbie attended Doreen Virtue's Angel Therapy Practitioner course in Laguna Beach, California, and she is now a certified ATP.

It is Debbie's intention to share hope, love and encouragement from the Angels with all who are open to receiving it.

Visit Debbie online at
www.LanguageofZibu.com

States

9 780979 830204